same
as
other
book

GREEK IMPERIALISM

BY

WILLIAM SCOTT FERGUSON

PROFESSOR OF ANCIENT HISTORY
HARVARD UNIVERSITY

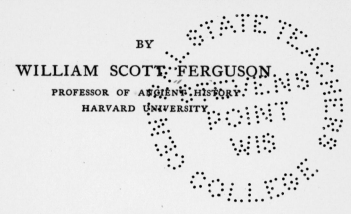

TOUT
BIEN OU
RIEN

BOSTON AND NEW YORK
HOUGHTON MIFFLIN COMPANY
The Riverside Press Cambridge

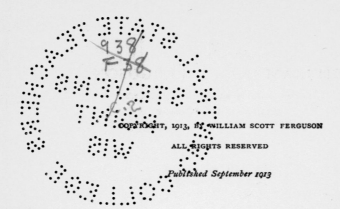

TO MY MOTHER

PREFACE

THIS book contains seven lectures, six of which were delivered at the Lowell Institute in Boston during February, 1913. In the first of them the main lines of imperial development in Greece are sketched. In the others I have tried to characterize, having regard rather to clearness than to novelty or completeness, the chief imperial growths which arose in Greece during the transformance of city-states from ultimate to constituent political units. I hope that these discussions of the theory and practice of government in the empires of Athens, Sparta, Alexander, the Ptolemies, Seleucids, and Antigonids will be found useful by the general reader, and especially by the student of politics and history. The idea I wish particularly to convey, however, is that there was continuity of constitutional development within the whole period. The city-state, indeed, reached its greatest efficiency in the time of Pericles, but the federation of city-states was being still perfected two hundred years afterwards. In government, as in science, the classic period was but the youthful bloom of Greece, whereas its vigorous maturity — in which it was cut down by Rome — came in the Macedonian time.

Briefly stated, my thesis is this: The city-states of
Greece were unicellular organisms with remarkable
insides, and they were incapable of growth except by
subdivision. They might reproduce their kind indefinitely, but the cells, new and old, could not combine to
form a strong nation. Thus it happened that after
Athens and Sparta had tried in vain to convert their
hegemonies over Greece into empires, a cancerous condition arose in Hellas, for which the proper remedy was
not to change the internal constitutions of city-states,
as Plato and Aristotle taught, but to change the texture
of their cell walls so as to enable them to adhere firmly
to one another. With a conservatism thoroughly in
harmony with the later character of the Greek people,
the Greeks struggled against this inevitable and salu-
tary change. But in the end they had to yield, saving,
however, what they could of their urban separateness,
while creating quasi-territorial states, by the use of the
federal system and deification of rulers. These two
contrivances were, accordingly, rival solutions of the
same great political problem. Nothing reveals more
clearly the limitations of Greek political theory than
that it takes no account either of them or of their
antecedents.

CAMBRIDGE, MASS., June, 1913.

CONTENTS

CONTENTS

GREEK IMPERIALISM

GREEK IMPERIALISM

I

IMPERIALISM AND THE CITY-STATE

IT is my purpose in this opening chapter to define some terms which I shall have to use repeatedly in the book; to make a somewhat detailed examination of the character of the Greek states whose political integrity was threatened by imperialism; to trace the development of imperialism to its culmination in the divine monarchy of Alexander the Great and his successors; and, at the same time, to arrange a general political setting for the topics to be discussed in the six succeeding chapters.

An empire is a state formed by the rule of one state over other states. It is immaterial in this connection what form of government the ruling people prefers. Power may be exercised there by a monarchy, an oligarchy, or a majority without altering in any essential the relation of the sovereign to its dependencies. Still less does it matter whether the subject people is governed by the one, the few, or the many; for all kinds of governments may exist, and have existed, in dependencies.

Naturally, an empire is compatible with any kind of an administrative service among both governors and governed. The suzerain may attend to its affairs with the aid of professional and specially trained officials, as in a bureaucracy; and a vassal may entrust the details of its public business to successive fractions of its citizens, as in some republics : no imperial relation is established unless separate states or parts of states are involved. But when these are related in a whole as superiors and inferiors, an empire at once arises.

The relation of inferiority and superiority is, however, essential in any empire. In modern times this is acknowledged with the utmost frankness. Upon the higher capacity for government claimed by the Christian peoples, the Western cultures, or the Anglo-Saxons, as the case may be, modern pride, greed, or conscience bases its right to control inferior races. "Take up the white man's burden" is the modern substitute for the ancient commandment, "Go ye into all the world and preach the Gospel to every creature." The possession of a better rule of public life imposes — it is affirmed — a missionary obligation no less weighty than the possession of a special rule of eternal life.

Less exasperating, perhaps, than this assumption of moral and political superiority is the candid profession of the right of the stronger. The right of conquest gives a title which is valid in international law when every other right is lacking. When superiority is stipulated to be absent, the product is a federation or something similar from which the name empire is withheld. When, in course of time, superiority dies out till a common right eventually embraces subject and sovereign alike, a new state arises, to which, as in the case of the present-day British world, the title empire is applied with some impropriety.

There is, however, still another kind of empire. In it the superior authority is not a people, but an individual. He is called an emperor, and his family a dynasty. His authority is bestowed, as the present German Emperor said at Königsberg in 1910, not by "parliaments, and meetings, and decisions of the peoples, but by the grace of God alone." He is "a chosen instrument of Heaven," to speak with the same high authority, and "goes his way without regard to the views and opinions of the day." An emperor, thus defined, is not properly a part of his state at all. He stands outside of it, and is equal or superior to it. He is a state unto himself; and his jurisdiction is not domestic but imperial, in that he exercises dominion over another state. *L'état c'est moi* is an imperfect definition of this kind of empire, however; for it presumes the absence of political organization and activity among the subjects of the emperor. It presumes the permanency of the condition of absolute surrender (*deditio*) which, with the Romans, prefaced the work of restoration — the reëstablishment of civil rights within an enlarged state. In actual experience, moreover, a complete autocracy never exists. The will of every emperor is bound by the legislation which he has himself enacted, or accepted with the throne from his predecessor. If responsible to nothing else, he is responsible to his own past. He may withdraw his charters: he cannot violate them with impunity.

The policy by which a people or an autocrat acquires and maintains an empire, we call imperialism. The term is, of course, a legacy from Rome — a mute witness to the peculiar importance of the Roman empire in the history of state-building. And, I suppose, it is the policy of Rome that we think of most instinctively when we allude to imperialism. This is by no means an accident. For not simply the type, but also many of the most noteworthy varieties of this kind of policy, are found in the experience of the Romans; and the course of political progress has been such that in the triumph of Rome imperialism reached its logical issue more closely than either before or since in the history of the world.

For the logical issue of a thoroughgoing imperial policy — one in which the possession of physical ability may be presupposed — is the formation of an universal empire. And, in fact, the two most powerful and ardent imperialists of antiquity, Alexander the Great and Julius Cæsar, aimed to include in their dominions the entire inhabitable world. This issue was, however, never more nearly reached than in the long period before and after the

Christian era during which only shifting nomads and intractable Parthians disputed successfully the will of the Roman Senate and the orders of the Roman emperors. For five hundred years after the triumph of Constantine the universality of the Roman empire was as mandatory in men's thinking as was the catholicity of the Christian Church. "There are many 'empires' in the world to-day," says Professor Bury[1] in explaining the coronation of Charlemagne in 800 A.D., "but in those days men could only conceive of one, the Roman *imperium*, which was simple and indivisible; two Roman empires were unimaginable. There might be more than the one emperor; but these others could only be legitimate and constitutional if they stood to him in a collegial relation." How thoroughly the Romans impressed the concept of universality upon the term empire may be judged by the fact that, in the face of all realities, the Frankish monarchs at Aachen and the Greek kings at Constantinople ruled as colleagues a Roman empire which stretched from the borders of Armenia to the shores of the Atlantic.

Transcendent as is the imperial achievement of the Romans, and unrivaled as is the political sagacity with which they consolidated their power and made it enduring, it must still be recognized that they were the heirs, in war, diplomacy, and government, of the Greeks, their predecessors. They worked with greater power and with

[1] *A History of the Eastern Roman Empire*, pp. 319 *f.*

larger units than did the Spartans and the Athenians. They benefited by the brilliant inventions and the costly errors of the Macedonians whose kingdoms they destroyed. But their success simply brought to a culmination the imperial movement in which Sparta, Athens, and Macedon were worthy co-workers. It is our task in this series of essays to examine in turn the imperial experiments by which the Greeks not only won a field for the display of their own talents, but also prepared the way for the unification of the ancient world in the empire of Rome.

I alluded a moment ago to the smallness of the units with which the imperial policy of Sparta and Athens had to deal. Before proceeding in the latter part of this chapter to trace the development of the forms by which imperialism was obscured, evaded, and ultimately justified in Greece, I should like to try to make clear the qualities which rendered the little Hellenic communities so hard for imperial digestion. In classic Greece, as in renascence Italy, the city was the state. It had not always been so; for in the past the land had been at one time in the possession of rudimentary nations, called *ethne*. But in the classic epoch these loose organisms persisted only in certain backward regions in the west and north. Elsewhere city-states had everywhere made their appearance as early as the sixth century B.C.

The circumstances in which these city-states arose are

shrouded in the mystery which surrounds most begin-
nings. They, accordingly, present all the better opportunity for the construction of a theory; and perhaps the
theory which had once the greatest vogue is that enun-
ciated by Fustel de Coulanges in his brilliant book on
The Ancient City. Of its main propositions, however,—
that each city-state came into being at a single moment;
that it was an artificial structure deliberately modeled
on the preëxistent family; that the family was a religious association created and organized for the worship
of ancestors; that the spirits of ancestors were the first
gods, or, indeed, were gods at all, — not one has stood
the test of a searching inquiry. On the contrary, it
seems established that the city-state was the result of a
natural growth, and that the incidents which accompanied its development, while varied and numerous,
were all manifestations of political progress. Growth in
the direction of a large number of distinct states was
natural in Greece in view of the well-known physical
features of the country; but the study of geography
does not explain why these states were cities. For the
true explanation of this phenomenon we must not con-
fine our observation to Greece. Broadly speaking, high
culture is everywhere city-bred, and the cities have
regularly been the leaders in political development. In
Babylonia that was the case, though the urban centres
there were dominated from a very early date by Semitic
tribes from the desert. Free cities, like Tyre and Sidon,

were the prime sources of Phœnician enterprise. The home of Roman law and government was a city, and when Italy led the world a second time, she was a complex of city-states. The Hanse towns and the Flemish communes, the chartered cities of England and France, acquired political liberty or political rights long before the rest of Central Europe. Where, in fact, the cities have not been the mother, and the territorial states simply the foster-mother, of freedom and culture, exceptional conditions have existed — such as the need of regulating the Nile's overflow in Egypt, and the model and influence of the Roman empire in Mohammedan and Christian Europe.

The city enables men to coöperate easily. In it ideas and feelings spread quickly. Life, property, and privileges are there protected by walls, and, if need be, by street barricades. "Two voices are there," wrote Wordsworth in 1807, his vision limited by the peril of England and Switzerland, —

> "one is of the sea,
> One of the mountains; each a mighty Voice:
> In both from age to age thou didst rejoice,
> They were thy chosen music, Liberty."

The voice of a city mob — that of Rome, Alexandria, Constantinople, Florence, or Paris, for example — was generally raucous and often cruel. But it made tyrants tremble and limited absolutism when the fear of assassination was powerless.

Fortunately, it is not with the origins, but with the characteristics, of the Greek city-states that we have to do mainly when we seek to discover the grounds of their hatred of all imperialistic projects. Let us, therefore, try to form a concrete impression of the salient features of the hundreds of little states with which the progressive parts of Greece were honeycombed at the beginning of the classic period, in the sixth century B.C. Each political cell, so to speak, had its nucleus in a walled town and its substance in a small circuit of grain, pasture, and garden land which the inhabitants of the town owned and cultivated. Most of the towns were simply hives of farmers. Whether the farmers were landlords, small proprietors, or peasants; however much they were divided by lines of social cleavage, they were all able to meet on the common ground of a single occupation. And every day from March to November, from the outcropping of the grass and foliage in the spring, through the season of the grain harvest, the vintage, and the picking of the olives, to the fall planting and seeding, the ebb and flow of agricultural life carried the population of the city to the country in the morning and back to the city again in the evening.

There were few towns in Greece whose land did not touch the sea; and from the sea another harvest was gathered. Fishing existed, of course; but that was not all. Transmarine commerce is never wholly absent in any maritime country. In Greece it was especially

favored by the difficulties of land transit, and by the
excellence of the highways which the sea laid while
carving the country up into a myriad of islands, head-
lands, and estuaries. Hence, by the opening of the sixth
century B.C. a second town had generally appeared on
the coast of each little state when the chief town had
developed, as was commonly the case, a few miles in-
land. In the new settlement the tone was set by the
sailor-folk and the traders; in the old centre by the
landed proprietors and the peasants. But the landlords
were frequently merchants, and the peasants could
easily attach work-places (*ergasteria*) to their houses —
which, though in the towns, were really farmhouses—
and become manufacturers in a small way; while it was
regularly the ambition of a trader or seaman to crown
a successful career by buying a farm, a ranch, or an
orchard. There was, accordingly, a very close connection between urban and agrarian pursuits and interests.

It is true that with the Greek occupation of the coasts
of the Mediterranean and Black Seas in the seventh
century B.C. some Greek towns, like Miletus, Samos,
Corinth, Ægina, Chalcis, and Eretria, became cities in
the modern sense of the term, with commercial and
industrial interests predominant. But even there the
advantages of urban life were within reach of the
farmers, as well as of the traders, artisans, and merchants, since all alike were residents of the city. The

only difference was that life in those cities was more rich and diversified than elsewhere.

The contrast between life in cities, with its complex social organization, its playhouses, its excitements, its stimuli to effort and to vice, its intolerance of oddities in manners and dress, and life in the country, with its simplicity which degenerates so easily into brutality, its monotony, its fanaticism in the pursuit of wealth, its contempt for the effeminacy of the shopkeeper, its piety and sobriety which easily accord with a longing to see the world and the wickedness thereof — this contrast which is so distressing an aspect of life in modern America, was almost entirely absent in classic Greece, at least among the enfranchised part of the population.

None of the cities was so large as to shut off the view of the country. After only a few minutes' walk Socrates and his companions might escape from the noise and confusion of Athens into the cool and fragrant groves of the suburbs. It was probably only into the biggest of the Greek cities that the olive trees and the grapevines did not push, as they and the late-come orange and lemon orchards push into the modern Greek hamlets. Even in Athens the crowing of the cock sounded the reveille for almost everybody, and it would never have come into the mind of an Athenian to suggest, as has been done in Boston, that a zoo should be stocked first with the common varieties of the domesticated animals. There is, says a French writer, a flavor of the barnyard about the comedies of Aristophanes. Yet this is the same Athens in which there were engaged in the building trades alone, according to Plutarch, carpenters, moulders, bronze-smiths, stone-cutters, dyers, veneerers in gold and ivory, painters, embroiderers, embossers; factors, sailors, pilots; wagon-makers, trainers of yoked beasts, drivers; rope-makers, weavers, cobblers, road-builders, and miners. This, too, is the Athens into which, as an ancient Athenian wrote, were swept, because of its maritime empire, the choice things of Sicily and Italy, of Cyprus, and Egypt, and Lydia, of Pontus and Peloponnesus, and many another place besides. When the farmer lived side by side in Athens, the largest city in the whole Greek world, with the trader and the artisan, the fusion of town and country must have been still more complete in the forty-three cities of Crete, the ten cities of Euboea, and the four cities of Ceos — an island only ten miles broad and fourteen long. This being the case, economic conditions tended to make the citizens of each state homogeneous to a degree foreign in modern experience; for, however rapid be its approach, the age has not yet arrived in America in which the "country is to be urbanized"; in which, to speak with a recent essayist,[1] farming is to be "of necessity a specialized department of urban life"; "the task of agricultural production is to be taken over by the classes of modern industrial organization; by the capitalist, the manager and

[1] *Atlantic Monthly*, Oct., 1912, vol. cx, pp. 517 *ff*.

the laborer"; in which "there is to be a continual shifting of laborers of the poorer classes back and forth between the town and the country," and "the distinction implied in the terms 'townsman' and 'countryman' is to be obliterated."

Whether our essayist be right or wrong in his forecast of the future of farming in America, we will not stop to discuss. It is enough to point out that the early age of Greece was such a one as he desiderates; that then life was exclusively and uniformly urban: with the result that the entire population of any given city-state could be regarded as merely a great family. And it not only could be, but it was in fact so regarded. Were not all citizens descendants of a common ancestor? This query aristocrats might answer in the negative, mindful of the special god or demigod of whom each nobleman thought himself the offspring. But his negative was generally qualified by the admission that he, too, if he were an Athenian, had Zeus and Apollo — Zeus of the homestead and Apollo of the fatherland — as his progenitors; that he, too, like all his fellow-citizens, was a descendant of Ion and a foster-child of Athena. The gods and goddesses of the Greeks were their creators in the literal physical sense of the word. Men projected backward, even to the age of the gods and heroes, with which the world began, the fact of paternity to which all animal origins were attributable; and since each city had its peculiar demigods, from which its citizens were directly

sprung, all its inhabitants were bound to one another by a peculiar tie of blood.

The family aspect of the Greek city is accentuated by
the fact that the town hall was a town hearth; that the
chief subdivisions of citizens were brotherhoods, and
that all permanent associations of them for public purposes assumed the descent of their several members
from common ancestors, who were naturally gods or
demigods. When heroes had to be discovered, with the
help of the Pythian prophetess, to act as progenitors for
the groups of citizens artificially united in the new electoral divisions which Clisthenes established in Athens in
508 B.C., it is conceivable that popular regard for purity
of stock helped Pericles to enact the notorious law of 451
B.C. limiting citizenship at Athens to those sprung from
the legitimate union of Athenian parents. Every city in
Greece inherited from its distant tribal past a strong
feeling of the kinship of its inhabitants, in comparison
with which the sense of ethnic and racial unity was weak
and watery. To destroy the political identity of a city
was like taking human life.

We must make allowance, moreover, in appraising the
strength of local attachments among both Greeks and
Romans, for their beliefs as to the fate of the dead. The
ancient world, like modern Japan, was saturated with
the idea that the spirits of departed ancestors needed the
ministrations of the living. Without the meat and drink
which the relatives brought to the grave; without the

coins — or the articles of use and pleasure which money might buy —that were buried with the body; without the covering of earth that was strewn over the dead, loved ones might lack life altogether in the underworld, or might lack everything that made the spirit life tolerable. "The beasts of the field and the birds of the air," rang the impassioned plea of Tiberius Gracchus[1] in introducing his agrarian reforms, "have their holes and their hiding-places, but the men who fight and die for Italy enjoy but the blessings of light and air. Our generals urge their soldiers to fight for the graves and the shrines of their ancestors. The appeal is idle and false. You cannot point to a paternal altar. You have no ancestral tomb. No! you fight and die to give wealth and luxury to others. You are called the masters of the world: yet there is no clod of earth that is really yours." Plutarch, with a touch which shows that despite his modernity he belongs to the civilization which he interprets, tells us that the Athenians before Salamis were disposed to count victory dear which was purchased by the desertion of the temples and the tombs of their fathers. No man who neglected the plot where his dead lay might hold the chief magistracies in Athens. The soil of his fatherland was thus in a peculiar sense holy ground to the citizen of a Greek city. He might leave it, but not to an enemy; and if he were, like Æneas, the last of his family, he was expected to carry his Lares and

---

[1] Plutarch, *Ti. Gracch.* 9; cf. Greenidge, *A History of Rome*, p. 111.

Penates with him. Into a pit dug on the new site every companion of Romulus, we are told in a legend which merely transfers into the past later-day practice, threw a morsel of earth brought from his old home land. This he did not simply from an intensification of the feeling which led the Scotch girl in the well-known ballad to take with her, when starting for America, not baggage, but sods from her mother's grave. He did it from the sentiment which led General Nogi the other day to provide for the spirits of his ancestors before committing suicide. Thereby the colonist brought his dead along with him to the new city. The Greeks and the Romans had, accordingly, a very special reason for local patriotism. Like the Hebrew Christians, they were "also compassed about with so great a crowd of witnesses."

We have made our peace with economics by considering first the effect of occupation and residence in giving to the citizens of each city-state solidarity of interest and attitude. We have dwelt a little on the force which beliefs as to their origin and their destiny hereafter exerted in keeping the city-states apart. We have still to notice the centrifugal influence on the Greek race of their urban institutions and politics.

Each city in Greece had its own laws and customs. These were not, as with us, cold abstractions, but real, ever active, almost living, personal forces, moulding incessantly their subjects according to a given model. The citizens of each city had, in fact, a general family resemblance, due to the imprint set upon them by their social and political institutions. Cities acquired by this means clear-cut individualities which were capable of definition, not simply by narrating their history, but also in terms of physical, intellectual, and emotional qualities. We may illustrate this point by observing that the Hellenes created one literary type which we have not borrowed from them: they wrote the biographies of cities as well as of men. Their philosophers studied the effects upon urban character of climate, prevailing winds and pursuits, location with reference to the sun and the sea, contact with foreigners, and other similar agencies. They even had specifics which they prescribed for the physiological and pathological ills of cities, just as our sciolists, on a much more slender basis of facts, however, diagnose the diseases and classify the good and evil qualities of nations.

The truth is that cities meant to all the Greeks what (and much besides) the city and the nation combined mean to those of us who do not live in the country. They were the source and object at once of municipal and national pride. The problems which city-states had to consider and solve were not simply those in which good citizens find it so hard nowadays to develop a wholesome interest. Questions of police, education, public works, appointments; conflicts of racial, sectional, class, and religious ambitions; rivalries with neighboring cities for commercial, political, and cultural leadership — controversies of this order are common to all cities in all times and places. But the politics of the Greek cities had a high seriousness of their own. Each town had its own foreign policy to determine, its own army to train and direct, its own church to equip with shrines and deities, its own gods to honor with games and tragedies. Every move on the complex chessboard of the Mediterranean world might be pregnant with meaning to it. On one day it might decide that the time had come to seize some borderland in dispute with its immediate neighbors. On another it might conclude an alliance which imposed the obligation to wage a great war against frightful odds. On another the subject of voting might be the recognition of a new god or goddess, which, in fact, was often tantamount to a new creation. And in considering all these matters citizens were simply doing what their fathers and forefathers had done from time immemorial. Memories of great actions done in olden times were preserved by monuments of bronze or marble, and revived annually by appropriate ceremonies. Legend and fact, blended in an edifying tradition, — the repository of the yearnings and ideals of dead generations, — inspired the living to bear themselves worthily in all national crises. "Love thou thy land with love far-brought from out the storied past" was an admonition of which Greek cities of the classic epoch stood in little need. The mischief was that the land which they loved was not all Greece, but merely the territory of a single town.

The national fanaticism of the countries of modern Europe is probably more tolerant of foreign interference than was the passionate patriotism of the little urban units with which the imperial policy of Athens and Sparta had to deal.

If you were to look at a map of Greece which distinguished the states, and not the meaningless ethnical or tribal divisions of the people, you would observe that from the outset Sparta and Athens were destined to greatness, if by nothing else, by the size and material resources of their territories. They were, however, themselves city-states, and inferior to none in the strength with which they held to the conviction that no greater humiliation could befall them than to have to submit to the domination of another city or the will of a foreign lord. With what show of reason, therefore, could they adopt a policy of imperialism? They had to deal with Greeks, and not with barbarians. Hence they could not invoke in the interest of their ambition the convenient doctrine that inferior races need a political guardian.

In estimating the territory of Sparta we have included in it not simply the land of the citizens which the serfs or Helots tilled for them, but also the much larger, but less valuable, mass of enveloping land which belonged to the Periœcs; for the hamlets of the latter were really Spartan municipalities. It was, moreover, with the resources of the whole complex that Sparta held the

Peloponnesians united under her leadership for one hundred and eighty years (550–370 B.C.). On the other hand, it was with the combined strength of the Peloponnesians that Sparta broke up the Athenian empire in 405 B.C., and widened the area of her leadership so as to include all Hellas. Thereafter Sparta's Peloponnesian league was simply the core of a general Hellenic league. The question is: What position did Sparta occupy in it?

Her legal rights rested solely upon a treaty of alliance (*symmachia*) which she had struck with each city in the league. But there can be no doubt that she had often secured the treaty in the first place by force, and that she interfered thereafter in the local affairs of both the Peloponnesian and the other Hellenic allies in a way not provided by its stipulations. But, however outrageous her conduct might be in fact, it was never formally reprehensible so long as the interference achieved its object. This was to establish or maintain, first against tyranny, and later against democracy, an aristocratic government in the allied cities. Since the aristocrats were always in a minority, they were bound to invite Spartan intervention for their own defense. Hence it was only when they failed to retain control of the government that an ally could regard Sparta's intermeddling as anything but the welcome act of a friendly power. "Perhaps some one may expostulate," writes a pamphleteer in 400 B.C. while commending to his fellow-citizens of Larisa a proposal that they join the Hellenic

league;[1] "but Sparta sets up an oligarchy everywhere.
That is true. But it is such a one as we prayed and
yearned for for ages, and lost when we had enjoyed it for
but a brief moment. Just compare the oligarchy they
favor with the one we have already. Where is there a
city in their domain, be it ever so small, in which a third
of the population does not take part in public affairs?
It is not by the Lacedæmonians, but by fortune, that
those who have no arms or other capacity for public service are disfranchised. Their exclusion lasts only so long
as their political worthlessness. How do we stand by
comparison? It's my belief that were we to pray for a
constitution we would not ask the gods for a different
one from that which Sparta wishes." To even moderate
men who thought as this speaker did, unruly Spartan
garrisons seemed quite compatible with local autonomy.
They came to Larisa at the call of the home authorities
and remained at the disposal of those who called them.
Their captains, the long-haired harmosts, took orders
and did not give them. Their presence involved no suspension of the constitution, no violation of the laws, no
seizure of public revenues. Naturally, the two thirds
who were disfranchised thought differently; but it is a
good rule of international law that a foreign state deal
with the Government, and not with the Opposition. The

---

[1] ['Hρώδου], Περὶ Πολιτείας, 30 (Ed. Drerup). With characteristic conservatism the English scholars, Adcock and Knox (*Klio*, 1913, pp. 249 *ff.*),
uphold the attribution of this pamphlet to Herodes Atticus.

mischief of this system, in the circumstances then exist-
ing in Greece, was that it bred civil war within the cities.
"War," says the Larisæan pamphleteer just quoted,
"is conceded to be the greatest of all evils by as much as
peace is the greatest of all blessings. Yet *stasis*, or civil
war, as far exceeds war in the magnitude of its evil as
war exceeds peace." The incentive to stasis was that
Athens, with a naval power as irresistible as was the land
power of Sparta, and an equally imposing array of allies,
had long continued to reach out a supporting or encouraging hand to the two thirds whom Sparta tried to keep
down. Athens, too, was the apostle of a great political
idea, "the constitutional equality of the many," and
whenever she succeeded in putting those who believed
in this creed in control of an allied city, or in keeping
them in control once they had the advantage, her interference was formally justifiable or at least justified. Not
she, but the government she upheld, had the responsibility.

With the outbreak of the great duel for national
leadership between Sparta and Athens which fills the
final third of the fifth century B.C., the war was carried
in the form of stasis into every city of the two confeder-
acies. For the leaders of both the one third and the two
thirds, says Thucydides in a famous passage of his history of the Peloponnesian War [1] "used specious names,

---

[1] Thucy., III, 82, 8. (The translation used here and elsewhere in the
book is that of Jowett.)

the one professing to uphold the constitutional equality of the many, the other the wisdom of an aristocracy, while they made the public interests, to which in name they were devoted, in reality their prize. Striving in every way to overcome each other, they committed the most monstrous crimes; yet even these were surpassed by the magnitude of their revenges, which they pursued to the very utmost, neither party observing any definite limits either of justice or public expediency, but both alike making the caprice of the moment their law. Either by the help of an unrighteous sentence, or grasping power with the strong hand, they were eager to satiate the impatience of party spirit. Neither faction cared for religion ; but any fair pretence which succeeded in effecting some odious purpose was greatly lauded. And the citizens who were of neither party fell a prey to both; either they were disliked because they held aloof, or men were jealous of their surviving. Thus stasis gave birth to every form of wickedness in Greece."

The singleness of purpose with which Sparta made vocational training the aim of her public education achieved the happy result that she had no men of letters to betray to posterity damaging secrets of state. Hence no one has done for her what Thucydides has done for Athens: let us have an insight into the conscience of the city at the time of its greatness. With brutal candor Cleon and others in Thucydides' narrative brush aside the formal justification of the Athenian empire and lay bare the fact that it was in reality a tyranny, a sovereignty exercised without a moral sanction, one which self-respecting people had a solemn duty to overthrow. "You should remember," said Cleon to the Athenians in 427 B.C.,[1] "that your empire is a despotism exercised over unwilling subjects who are always conspiring against you; they do not obey in return for any kindness which you do them to your own injury, but in so far as you are their mistress; they have no love of you, but they are held down by force."

Dependence upon Sparta or Athens was, in fact, regarded by none of their allies except as the less of two evils: the greater was dependence upon their domestic foes. Hence the tyranny just described did not arise with the consent of the tyrannized. The allies of Athens had consented to enter only into alliance (symmachia) with her on stipulated terms and for a stipulated purpose — protection against Persia. What they had neglected to stipulate was the time for which they were to remain allies. Athens, accordingly, denied them the right to secede, and when particular cities tried none the less to withdraw, she made the preservation of the union a moral ground for coercion, and with the aid of such cities as remained faithful, and the fleet which she kept ready for action by the financial contributions of all, she forced them back on terms such as a conqueror could dictate. A new treaty of alliance was, however, the

[1] Thucy., III, 37, 2.

future, as it had been the ancient, tie. And speaking broadly, we may affirm that in the city-state world of classic Greece an empire was legally impossible: what we, and the ancients, looking to realities, call an empire was an aggregate knit together by treaties, the very formation of which shows that we have to do, not with a single sovereign, but with a group of sovereigns. In other words, the city remained the ultimate political unit. The rule of Athens and Sparta was, strictly speaking, an hegemony and not an *arche;* a shifting and temporary leadership, and not a permanent suzerainty. It was a necessity of circumstances assumed to be exceptional.

Unfortunately, experience showed that the circumstances in which imperialism was a political necessity recurred constantly. After the fall of Athens in 404 B.C., a defensive war against the barbarians — the Macedonians in Thessaly, the Persians in Ionia — served as a justification to Sparta in employing force to maintain the hegemony which she had won. But in 387 B.C. the peace known as the "King's Peace," or the "Peace of Antalcidas," was concluded with Persia, whereupon it became impossible to use any longer the national cause as even a pretext for tyranny. The hegemony, however, was not abandoned. It had to be maintained, it was alleged, to keep the other cities free, and to this end Persia lent aid to Sparta and Thebes successively. If an empire could only be prevented by an empire, and national recreancy to boot, the times were surely out of joint. Such an issue was the *reductio ad absurdum* of the system of hegemonies, as both reformers and statesmen in Greece came speedily to realize.

The reformers strove to alter the untoward circumstances, and in a later chapter we shall have occasion to note how Plato and Aristotle, with a blind faith in the power of education and of legislation, aimed to divert citizens from work to leisure and from war to peace, and both to eradicate the greed for land and money and to restrict the natural increase of population to which they traced the imperialistic spirit. Some of the statesmen followed their lead. Others, however, conceding that unity was demanded for the preservation and spread of civilization, and that the world needed not fewer but more Greeks, either, like the great publicist Isocrates, advocated an hegemony on the old lines but endowed with stability through being based on general consent, or favored one of several new devices for welding cities into a permanent territorial state. Respect for progress bids us to view at this point somewhat narrowly these unitarian movements.

The position attained by Thebes in Greece after her victory over Sparta at Leuctra in 371 B.C. was simply an hegemony of the earlier model — the reoccupation of lines proved twice already to be untenable.[1] On

---

[1] The same is true of the second Athenian empire. The confederation from which it grew had no reason to outlast the occasion which had called

the other hand, the position occupied by Thebes in Bœotia prior to 387 B.C. was clearly anticipatory of what the future was to bring to Greece as a whole. Bœotia was thereby blocked off into six districts,[1] one (Thebes) with four electoral divisions, two (Orchomenus and Thespiæ) with two each, and three with one apiece. Six of the ten city-states of Bœotia—the six little lake cities—were confined to two of the eleven divisions. This was a setback to them and a boon to Thebes, seeing that each division furnished one of the eleven Bœotarchs who formed the executive of the league, sixty of the six hundred and sixty councillors who formed the Bœotian synod, and its corresponding share of the league judges. Thebes thus became the Prussia of Bœotia, and in return for the political advantages which it gained and four elevenths of the revenues which it received, it undertook to provide four elevenths of the soldiers and four elevenths of the taxes. In this way the burdens and the advantages of the league were distributed according to the population and wealth of the different parts of the country. That was equitable; and since the city-states, though thrust into the background and held responsible for decisions in the making of which they had often little influence, formed a single *ethnos* and spoke a single dialect, they were evidently

it into existence—the "tyranny" of Sparta. It was, therefore, by design at least, a temporary, and not a permanent, union.

[1] *Hellenica Oxyrhyn.*, 11, 2–4.

fairly well satisfied. As the league was constituted, Thebes was forced to struggle with Orchomenus and Thespiæ for the control of the six little lake cities. In this she was normally successful — so successful, in fact, that in 387 B.C. Sparta, while enforcing the King's Peace, dissolved the league in order to destroy her influence. It was not revived when Thebes reunited Bœotia (377–371 B.C.), and under Epaminondas we may more properly speak of Bœotia as a single city-state like Attica than as a league of city-states.

᾿ Though sacrificed at home to the ambition of Thebes, the Bœotian league maintained a high prestige abroad. Some of its institutions had been transferred to Athens during the revolution of 411 B.C., and others had been adopted in Arcadia after they had been set aside in Bœotia. Moreover, and this is an important historical connection which the wonderful epigraphical researches of Adolph Wilhelm [1] enable us to establish, the Bœotian league reappears *mutatis mutandis* in the organization imposed upon all Greece by Philip of Macedon after his crowning victory at Chæronea in 338 B.C. For if we equate Philip and the Committee of Public Safety with the eleven Bœotarchs, the synod of Corinth with the Bœotian synod of six hundred and sixty, and the districts into which Hellas, including Macedon and excluding only Sparta, was divided for federal pur-

[1] *Attische Urkunden*, I Teil. (Sitzb. d. Akad. in Wien. Phil.-hist. Klasse. 165, 6, 1911).

poses, with the six districts which had existed in Bœotia, it is evident that the political system used by Philip for organizing the Greeks was borrowed from Bœotia no less than the military system with which he conquered them. It was not for nothing that the king of Macedon had spent his youth as a hostage in Thebes.

Characteristic of the Bœotian league and of Philip's Hellenic league is the synod. It was in each a strictly representative body. Its members were apportioned to the area constituting the league in such a way that the larger states had several representatives and the smaller states had one representative between them; while in the Hellenic league neighboring states and federated states were treated as a unit and given proportional representation. That this made all but the largest state — Macedon — the largest state's inferiors and subordinated many city-states to the federal districts to which they belonged, is obvious. And in this case loss of local liberty was compensated for very imperfectly by the consideration that what the constituent states surrendered the Hellenic synod, which met at Corinth, gained. The national appeal was far weaker than the ethnic appeal had been in Bœotia. The liberty lost had indeed been a bane and not a blessing. After 338 B.C. the cities could no longer enjoy the excitement of waging private wars and fomenting revolutions. No longer were they free to be enemies of Philip. Henceforth they must contribute the quota of horsemen, hoplites, light-armed troops, and sailors for which their representation in the synod obligated them, or pay a heavy fine for every day their contingents were absent from the national levy. The synod completed its organization by choosing Philip its *hegemon* by land and sea, and selected as its executive board a Committee of Public Safety which seemingly had its sessions at Pydna. The committee the confederates probably welcomed as a possible champion of their interests. The unwelcome organ of the league, and the one for which there was no parallel in Bœotia, was the hegemon. Subordination to a synod was offensive enough to city-states which regarded complete independence as alone ideal. It was intolerable to them to submit to a synod which its hegemon, Philip of Macedon, controlled, — one which could never have any one but the contemporary king of Macedon as its hegemon. The hegemony of Macedon was sugar-coated, but it was none the less an hegemony, and, as such, illegal and unacceptable.[1]

A notable start in the direction of uniting city-states legally in a larger whole had been made by Athens during the epoch of her empire. She had then founded many colonies (*cleruchies*), which, though organized as separate cities, retained for their residents citizenship in Athens. Why not grant citizenship (*polity*) to the inhabitants of other cities as well? There were some, and

---

[1] It was revived on much less objectionable terms by Antigonus Doson. See below, page 34 and chapter VII.

among them the comedian Aristophanes,[1] who can-
vassed this idea. "Let us assume," he says, "that our
city is a heap of wool, and that each of our allied cities is
a fleck of wool. Let us take all the wool and spin it into
yarn, and weave the yarn into a great blanket with
which to protect our lord Demos against the cold." But
for this drastic measure the times were not ripe. It was
altogether repugnant to the pride of the Athenians to
share with everybody advantages which they had sacrificed so much to acquire; and there was little in the
advantages thus diluted to compensate other cities for
the at least partial loss of identity which they were
bound to sustain on acquiring Athenian citizenship. In
the one instance in which this course was taken, the
Samians, to whom Athens gave her full civic rights in
the supreme agony of the Peloponnesian War, had both
earned them and come to appreciate them by sacrificing
their own territory rather than desert their ally.

Another less heroic expedient for bringing about a permanent *entente* between cities was the grant of *isopolity*,
or reciprocity of citizenship. In certain cases this was
the concession of the passive rights of citizenship
(*civitas sine suffragio*) to all citizens of a particular city
who should take up residence in, or even merely visit,
the territory of the grantor. Thus circumscribed, however, it amounted simply to an exchange of commercial
privileges, and proved barren of political consequences

[1] *Lysistrata*, 579 *ff.*

in that each city reserved to itself complete control of its own policy, thus rendering impossible any advance in state building. It remained for the Romans to render this institution fruitful to an astonishing degree by making the legal exercise of Roman citizenship independent of migration to Rome.

Substantially the same result was achieved by the Greeks through what they termed *sympolity*, or joint citizenship. This was possessed from of old by rudimentary nations, like the Achæans and the Ætolians,[1] among whom the towns and hamlets had never become independent and self-sufficient political units; so that the inhabitants were Achæans from Ægium, or Achæans from Cerynia, or Achæans from some other of the ten so-called cities of which the Achæan nation or league was constituted. In like fashion the Ætolian hamlets had a double citizenship. An essential part of this scheme, evidently, was that each city had an equal voice in the election of the officials of the league and in the settlement of all federal matters. And so satisfactory a safeguard of urban autonomy did this prove to be that in the last half of the third century B.C. city after city in the Peloponnesus outside the ancient limits of Achæa took the irrevocable step of acquiring Achæan citizenship in addition to its own; while in Central Greece the Ætolians by fair means or foul bestowed a dual citizenship upon all their neighbors. Athens and Sparta

[1] See below, chapter VII.

alone persisted in their isolation, the former on the strength of an international guarantee of autonomy, the latter in stubborn reliance upon its own powers. The other city-states entrusted to an international board, not for a definite or indefinite term of years, but for all future time, complete control of their foreign relations. Each city put permanently the international authority between itself and the outside world, thus escaping individual danger by the surrender of individual diplomacy.[1]

In this way arose what by the general consent of historians and jurists is the most perfect state which antiquity produced. The antinomy between the city-state and the imperial spirit which had existed for centuries was reduced to a minimum by the nice balance of the federal system.

There were defects in the Achæan and Ætolian leagues which their statesmen did not remove. "Equality," says Aristotle, "is just, but only between equals." The cities which had an equal voice in the international board, like the modern nations which cast a vote each at the Hague Congress, were unequal in population and in wealth.

The Achæans and Ætolians came nearer than any ancient republicans to entrusting power to representatives; but, besides creating a large legislative council, constituted in successive years, in the one case, of dif-

[1] See below, chapter VII.

ferent fractions of the citizens of each city, and in the
other, of deputies apportioned to the constituent cities
according to their size, they showed the ingrained distrust held by all Greeks for oligarchy by requiring the
reference to a general assembly of all matters of high
importance.

How to satisfy the just claims of those whom distance
or lack of leisure prevented from coming to the meeting-
place, they did not discover.

However, it was not these institutional imperfections
which prevented the unification of Hellas in a single
federation. For this result could not now be achieved
by any triumph of political science. Antigonus Doson
(229–221 B.C.) whose name ought not to be unknown
where Callicratidas, Agesilaus, Iphicrates, and Phocion
are household words, attempted with equal skill and
generosity to combine the new federal idea with the old
idea of a representative national congress meeting at
Corinth under the hegemony of the king of Macedon;[1]
but the best that can be said of the combination he made
is that despite its great promise and possibilities it
proved unacceptable to Hellas, and hence ineffective.[2]
The situation had now got beyond the control of the
Greek people. It may, perhaps, be realized best, if we
imagine that the European nations of to-day, weakened politically by continuous emigration and incessant
conflicts, economically, by the withdrawal of industry

[1] See above, page 30.   [2] See below, chapter VII.

and commerce to more favorably situated districts under European control, let us say in the East, were to pool their diplomatic and military interests, and entrust them, not to a European parliament, but to warring Latin and Teutonic parliaments, and were to take this step only to escape the Russian peril and when America was already thundering at their shores, if that be imaginable, coming with irresistible might, at once to save and to destroy.

To describe how the Roman republic emancipated Greece from Macedon, impressed her will upon the Greek kingdoms of the East, and built up a universal empire of diverse fragments, lies beyond the scope of this book. We may note simply that to some cities she gave her citizenship, or polity, thus destroying their identity altogether; that to others she gave isopolity, or reciprocity of citizenship, and with it the local advantages preserved in Greece by sympolity, or joint citizenship, thus creating the municipality and organizing wards, so to speak, of the city of Rome all over Italy; that some (the *socii*, or Italian allies) she bound to herself by irrevocable treaties till she was forced to give them municipal status, and others (the "friends," *amici*, or the "friends and allies," *amici et socii*, in what later became the provinces) by understandings or temporary treaties till she had familiarized herself with deification of rulers, which was the Greek method of legalizing absolutism.

A word on this strange institution and I have finished

this survey of the expedients devised by the Greeks to obscure, evade, and finally to justify imperialism. The Greek method of legalizing despotism was Alexander the Great's genial adaptation to state building of an idea which his tutor, Aristotle, had developed in his *Politics*.[1] It was a means of uniting cities or provinces in an indissoluble whole while preserving, on the one hand, the superiority and freedom of action of the suzerain, be it an emperor or a republic, and, on the other hand, the self-respect of the inferior states, without which their status was politically intolerable. Deification of rulers did the impossible: it reconciled completely the antinomy between the city-state and imperialism. It resolved the antagonism into two harmonious duties; the duty of the ruler to command and of the subject to obey.

To Alexander the Great governments have been in serious debt for over two thousand years. From him to Kaiser Wilhelm II runs an unbroken line. So long as the world had many gods and did not believe in the supernatural power of any of them, there was no religious difficulty in adding to its stock another such deity in the person of the living monarch. With the decadence of polytheism, however, a slight change was necessary. In Constantine's time god-kings suffered the same fate as other pagan gods; but with a difference. The heathen gods became devils or were metamorphosed into saints.

[1] See especially Ed. Meyer, *Kleine Schriften*, 283 *ff*., and below, chapter IV.

The kings became men chosen for their high office by God, Most High. Crowned, usually by their predecessors, and anointed by God's priests, the patriarchs, they governed by divine right and acknowledged responsibility only to their Creator.[1] In a less ecclesiastical world, as in modern Prussia, the kings crown themselves. But with these later developments we have no concern in this book. I shall endeavor, however, in chapters III–VI, to trace the growth of deification in the world-monarchy of Alexander the Great, and to make clear the purpose it served in the empires of the Ptolemies and Seleucids.

SELECT BIBLIOGRAPHY

1. DE COULANGES, FUSTEL. *La cité antique* [7] (1879).
2. BUSOLT, G. *Die griechischen Staats- und Rechtsaltertümer*,[2] (1892). In Müller's *Handbuch der klassischen Altertumswissenschaft*, IV, I.
3. SCHÖMANN-LIPSIUS. *Griechische Alterthümer*,[4] II (1892).
4. FRANCOTTE, H. *La Polis grecque* (1907).
5. WILAMOWITZ-MOELLENDORFF, ULRICH VON. *Staat und Gesellschaft der Griechen* (1910). In Hinneberg's *Die Kultur der Gegenwart*. Teil II, Abteilung IV, I.
6. ZIMMERN, ALFRED. *The Greek Commonwealth* (1911).
7. KEIL, BRUNO. *Griechische Staatsaltertümer* (1912). In Gercke and Norden's *Einleitung in die Altertumswissenschaft*, pp. 297 *ff.*

[1] Bury, J. B., *The Constitution of the Later Roman Empire* (1910), pp. 10 *ff.*, 36.

II

ATHENS: AN IMPERIAL DEMOCRACY

No form of government, or profession of political idea, saves a state from imperialism. Even this country, which is dedicated, as is no other of the modern great powers, to the concept of popular sovereignty; which uprears the structure of its state upon a belief in the essential equality of men, and treats, or at least aims to treat, as comparatively negligible the differences created by birth and race, education and religion, property and occupation;—even this idealistic republic has become an empire in our own time and almost without our perceiving it. M. Bouché-Leclercq has given a prominent place in his *Leçons d' histoire romaine* [1] to the discomforting doctrine that the Romans conquered the world in spite of themselves — a debatable question, as he himself shows. It is not our sense of truth that is gratified when we are told that the beatitude, "Blessed are the meek, for they shall inherit the earth," designates the English. Yet Seeley has maintained the thesis that the British empire was secured in a "prolonged fit of national absence of mind." Unwittingly, it seems, the modern foster-mother of liberal institutions has become the mistress of countless millions.

[1] Pages 27 *ff.*

There never was a people which made the principle that all its citizens were equal a more live reality than the Athenians made it; and no state to my knowledge was more cunningly contrived to insure the government of the people than was theirs. Yet they became imperialists with ardor and conviction, and with this much of logical consequence, that, while they believed in democracy for everybody, they did not doubt that the Athenians had earned the right to rule both Greeks and barbarians by the acquisition of superior culture. Equality among its citizens Athens carefully distinguished from equality among all men.

The foundations of Athenian democracy and empire were laid by Themistocles, whose figure moves weird and gigantic through the golden mist in which Herodotus has enveloped the great Persian War. And it was this genial statesman, to whose unerring skill in discerning the course of coming events the austere historian Thucydides pays a rare tribute, who mapped out for his city the foreign policy by which it had the best chance of realizing its imperial ambition. Let it use its great fleet, which by fifteen years of persistent advocacy he had led the Athenians to build, as its arm of offense, and its impregnable walls, which he had enabled the Athenians to construct despite the treacherous opposition of Sparta, as a bulwark of defense and a basis for timely advance against its powerful continental rivals. Let it utilize the wave of democratic fervor then sweeping through Greece to consolidate its power within the Confederacy of Delos and to undermine and eventually to overthrow the leadership which Sparta, by the support of dying mediæval aristocracies, had hitherto possessed in Hellenic affairs. Let it make peace on advantageous terms with Persia; use the liberty thus secured to break the power of Sparta, and, on the basis of a consolidated Hellas, strike boldly for Athenian dominion of the world.

It seems almost incredible that a clear-headed man should have entertained a programme of such magnitude. But we must remember that never had human beings more clearly performed the obviously miraculous. *We* know, on the authority of a German military expert,[1] that, had the host which followed Xerxes to Athens numbered the 5,283,220 men attributed to it by Herodotus "without taking count of women cooks, concubines, eunuchs, beasts of burden, cattle, and Indian dogs," its rear guard must have been still filing out of Sardis while its van was vainly storming Thermopylæ. But what Herodotus reports is what the Athenians believed. They had met and routed the might of all Asia. They had mastered in fair fight the conquerors of all other peoples. The world was theirs: it was merely a question of taking possession.

Themistocles had, accordingly, to reckon with a

---

[1] Delbrück, *Die Perserkriege und die Burgunderkriege*, pp. 137 *ff.*; Beloch, *Griechische Geschichte*, I (1893), p. 368, n. 3.

national self-confidence which knew no bounds. And this had been increased by famous victories of Cimon over the Persians, and a revolt of the Helots which disclosed the fatal weakness of Sparta, when in 461 B.C. the task of conducting the fierce current of national energy, first for fifteen years (461–446 B.C.) in a heroic, but fruitless, struggle by sea and land against the Greeks and Persians simultaneously, and then for fifteen further years (446–431 B.C.) in the prosecution of glorious works of peace, fell upon the broad shoulders of Pericles, Xanthippus's son.

It is conceded that there is no taskmaster so ruthless as one's own will. The impulse to action during this strenuous epoch came from the Athenian people itself, not from its chief statesman. That fact does not, however, diminish the credit of Pericles. The golden age of Greece is, properly speaking, a golden age of Athens, and to its birth many things contributed; but decisive among them, in addition to the intensity of national life already alluded to, was an unrivaled facility for great leaders to get into effective contact with the masses under conditions in which there was the fullest opportunity for men in general to use their natural powers to the utmost. This happy combination of creative genius and receptive multitude arose in the main from the democratic institutions of Athens; but, for the public and private wealth without which Athenian democracy proved unworkable, and for the imaginative stimulus which enterprises of great pitch and moment alone give, the possession of empire was, perhaps, essential.

In the age of Pericles, Athens was a city with a population of about 150,000. Attica, the territory of the Athenians, had an approximately equal number of inhabitants. Of the 300,000 thus accounted for, about one third was servile and one sixth foreign. The free and franchised population made up one half of the total, and yielded about 50,000 males of military age.

The empire of the Athenians consisted of five provinces, the Thracian, Hellespontine, Insular, Ionian, and Carian, with a total population of perhaps, 2,000,000. It formed a complex of islands, peninsulas, and estuaries, the most remote extremities of which were distant two hundred or two hundred and fifty miles from Athens. The highways of this empire were the land-locked channels and lakes which make up the Ægean Archipelago. Their greatest length in normal circumstances was a continuous voyage of about eight days. On the other hand, no land way of more than a single day's march need be traversed by an Athenian expedition aimed at any of its subject cities. Without the control of the sea the empire was, accordingly, unthinkable. This absent, the district fell at once into more than four hundred fragments, the thousand "cities" from which, according to the comedian Aristophanes, the Athenians gathered tribute.

The Athenian sphere of naval operations and of political and commercial interests reached far beyond the frontiers of the empire. It included points like Sicily, Egypt, Phœnicia, and the Euxine, distant over six hundred miles from the Piræus. An Athenian fleet might thus require the best part of a month to reach its destination. The world which had to take careful account of the Athenian naval power in all its political and military calculations, the world which Athens under Pericles sought to dominate, must have had a population of over 20,000,000.

If, then, we take into account the ratio of dominant, subject, and foreign elements, and also the time consumed in reaching with ships, orders, or explanations, the outer limits of authority, the magnitude of Athens's imperial undertaking will stand comparison with that of England in modern times.

In Sparta the gravestone of a citizen was inscribed regularly with his name alone. No epitaph was needed there to tell the tale of a life; for the life of one citizen was the well-known life of all. If, however, a man had died for his country, two words, ἐν πολέμῳ, "in war," expressed with laconic brevity his ground of distinction.

For those who fell in battle Athens set apart a public cemetery near the Dipylon Gate, and at the end of every campaign a commemorative service was held there in honor of the year's crop of martyrs. A man high in public esteem voiced the nation's gratitude for the sacrifice. On such an occasion, at the end of the first year of the Peloponnesian War, Pericles reversed the normal procedure, and, instead of expatiating on the merits of the fallen, he explained in an eloquent speech why Athens was worthy of loyalty unto death. Thucydides heard his words, and, perhaps many years afterwards, reproduced them as best he could in the famous *Funeral Oration*.

The statesman did not linger long over the legendary glories of Athens. Her alleged boons to humanity — grain, the norms of civilized life, the drama; the services, that is to say, upon which the later Athenians dwelt with special pride — had no meaning for him. Two things their ancestors had done: they had defended their country successfully, and had transmitted to their descendants a free state. "And if these were worthy of praise," [1] proceeds his splendid exordium, "still more were our fathers, who added to their inheritance, and after many a struggle transmitted to us their sons this great empire. And we ourselves assembled here to-day, who are still most of us in the vigor of life, have chiefly done the work of improvement, and have richly endowed our city with all things, so that she is sufficient for herself both in peace and war. Of the military exploits by which our various possessions were acquired, or of the energy with which we or our fathers

[1] Thucy., II, 36, 2.

drove back the tide of war, Hellenic or Barbarian, I will not speak; for the tale would be long and is familiar to you. But . . . I should like to point out by what principles of action we rose to power, and under what institutions and through what manner of life our empire became great."

In these words of Pericles I should like you to find stated the theme of my second chapter. And were it not that Pericles left unexplained, what the Athenians whom he addressed knew without explanation, the social and political forms by which they realized their ideals, I might absolve my task by one long quotation. I might transcribe the whole *Oration* and have done with it.

That being inexpedient, I cannot do better than present, using again Pericles's own words as a sort of text, the main principles of Athenian policy. But in passing I may be permitted to observe that were our knowledge of Athens dependent solely upon the *Funeral Oration;* had we to form our idea of political life in fifth-century B.C. Greece from it alone, we might still infer a unique epoch in the history of mankind. Fortunately, that is not the case. The "tooth of time and razure of oblivion" have spared the Parthenon and its matchless sculptures, the noble tragedies of Æschylus and Sophocles, and the undying charm of Herodotus. Ideals are always grounded in some measure in realities. At the least they stand to them as the "perfect round"

to the "broken arc." Even in Plato's psychology the
mind needs to be sharpened by observation and reflec-
tion before, as in a flash of light, the glimpse of the
divine idea suddenly appears. Hence, were the affirma-
tions of the *Funeral Oration* unsupported by contemporary monuments of similar spirit, they would still be
helpful revelations of Athenian democracy. And this
conclusion, as I hope to show, rests not upon logical
inference alone, but also upon the evidence of minute
research.

"It is true," said Pericles,[1] "we are called a democracy,
for the administration is in the hands of the many and
not of the few. But while the law secures equal justice
to all alike in their private disputes, the claim of excellence is also recognized, and when a citizen is in any
way distinguished, he is preferred to the public service,
not as a matter of privilege, but as the reward of merit.
Neither is poverty a bar, but a man may benefit his
country whatever be the obscurity of his condition.
There is no exclusiveness in our public life, and in our
private intercourse we are not suspicious of one another,
nor angry with our neighbor if he does what he likes;
we do not put on sour looks at him which, though harmless, are not pleasant. While we are thus unconstrained in
our private intercourse, a spirit of reverence pervades
our public acts; we are prevented from doing wrong by

[1] Thucy., ii, 37 *ff*.

respect for authority and for the laws, having an especial
regard to those ordained for the protection of the injured
as well as to those unwritten laws which bring upon the
transgressor of them the reprobation of the general sentiment. . . . Wealth we employ not for talk and ostenta-
tion, but when there is a real use for it. To avow poverty with us is no disgrace: the true disgrace is in doing
nothing to avoid it. An Athenian citizen does not neglect the state because he takes care of his own household; and even those of us who are engaged in business
have a very fair idea of politics. We alone regard a man
who takes no interest in public affairs, not as a harmless
but as a useless character; and if few of us are origi-
nators, we are all sound judges of a policy. The great
impediment to action is, in our opinion, not discussion
but the want of that knowledge which is gained by discussion preparatory to action. For we have a peculiar
power of thinking before we act and of acting too. . . .
And we have not forgotten to provide for our weary
spirits many relaxations from toil; we have regular
games and sacrifices throughout the year; at home the
style of our life is refined; and the delight which we daily
feel in all these things helps to banish melancholy. Because of the greatness of our city the fruits of the whole
earth flow in upon us; so that we enjoy the goods of
other countries as freely as of our own. . . . We are
lovers of the beautiful, yet simple in our tastes, and we
cultivate the mind without loss of manliness. . . . To

sum up: I say that Athens is the school of Hellas, and
that the individual Athenian in his own person seems to
have the power of adapting himself to the most varied
forms of action with the utmost versatility and grace.
This is no passing and idle word, but truth and fact;
and the assertion is verified by the position to which
these qualities have raised the state. . . . And we shall
assuredly not be without witnesses; there are mighty
monuments of our power which will make us the wonder
of this and of succeeding ages; we shall not need the
praises of Homer or of any other panegyrist whose
poetry may please for the moment, although his representation of the facts will not bear the light of day. For
we have compelled every land and every sea to open a
path for our valor, and have everywhere planted eternal
memorials of our friendship and of our enmity."

Such were the proud claims of the great Athenian
statesman. Of art there was said no word except in so
far as art was embodied in the monuments of empire.
Music and the drama are alluded to, but in the same
breath with athletic contests, as the relaxation of over-
worked men. The speaker has no apology to make for
democracy. He gloried in imperialism. Had he met
Plato in Elysium — Plato who was born in the year after
Pericles's death, and both embodied and expressed the
higher ideals of a later generation of Athenians — he
would have disdained to reply to the philosopher's accu-

sation that he had filled the city with traders and shops and ships and dockyards and such rubbish, instead of with righteousness and justice.

Taking the *Funeral Oration* as my text, I should like to explain at this point by what institutions the principles of Periclean democracy and imperialism were converted into facts.

It was in the *ecclesia,* or general assembly, and in the *heliæa*, or popular courts of justice, that sovereign power was vested in Athens.[1] The heliæa demanded of its jurors only that they should be citizens in good standing, but each year it drew according to need from a specially constituted list of 6000. So, too, of the 50,000 citizens who might attend the ecclesia, 6000 were regarded as a quorum when a quorum was required, and commonly an even smaller number was present. Meetings of the ecclesia were held either in the city or at the harbor; hence the urban element tended to dominate. Stated meetings occurred four times a month, but others might be called by the generals or the council. Various panels of from 401 to 2001 jurymen each might be allotted to tribunals on every day of the year which was not set aside for a public festival or preëmpted by a meeting of the ecclesia. Usually poor men of advanced years, such as were unsuited for more active work and

[1] For the following sections see especially Aristotle's *Constitution of the Athenians.*

were satisfied with the indemnity of two obols [1] per day, volunteered for registration among the 6000 jurors.

The work of Parliament was divided between the ecclesia and the heliæa; for legislation in the strict sense of the term could be enacted only by the joint action of the two bodies.[2] Administrative decrees, moreover, by means of which the ecclesia disposed of all important public business, and which might differ from laws only in a formal way, could be suspended at the initiative of individuals and were incontestable only when passed on, as to constitutionality or public expediency, by the heliæa. The men who sat in the heliæa were but common citizens like those who voted in the ecclesia; but they came to sit in judgment on both laws and decrees by the accident of the lot and not because of any particular interest in the questions concerned. In other words, the courts could not be packed with partisans as the meetings of the ecclesia commonly were. This fact, together with the delay which necessarily occurred, protected the state against the verdict of a chance majority, which was in fact usually a minority of all the citizens. There was no such thing in Athens as the final settlement of controversial matters by a single popular vote.

The heliæa acted as sovereign in one further particular. Upon it devolved the duty of determining whether

[1] Seven cents, equal in purchasing power to thirty-five cents perhaps.
[2] Greenidge, *Greek Constitutional History* (1896), pp. 170 *ff*.

the magistrates and councilors observed the laws and conducted themselves honestly during their years of office. It was to the sworn assembly of the Athenians, accordingly, that all those engaged in civil administration were responsible. The ecclesia, on the other hand, had the right to impeach and dismiss those officials who, being given discretionary powers, abused them.

The main work of the heliæa was of course to settle domestic and imperial litigation. As we shall see, the judicial power of the heliæa gave it a large measure of political control over all the subject cities of Athens.

The heliæa was the brake on the democratic machine: the ecclesia was the dynamo. The intent of the Athenians was that all political decisions of importance should be reached, after full debate, by the ecclesia. It was, however, obvious that an assembly of from five to fifty thousand men would proceed with disastrous slowness if all matters, great and small, were laid before it, or even if it considered only significant affairs, but considered them without previous examination and formulation. Perversion of modern democracies results most notably from the usurpation of power on the part of those who sift proposals for popular reference. Athens had to guard against a similar danger. Hence the harbinger of democracy, Clisthenes, created for it one of the most peculiar *probuleutic*, or deliberative, bodies which ever had the handling of large affairs. This was the council of the Five Hundred.

It was constituted anew each year and was made an exact miniature of the ecclesia which it was to serve. Every ward and township of Attica, to the number of one hundred and over, first eliminated such of its members as had not yet reached their thirtieth year or had already served two terms in the council, and then selected by lot from among the rest the councilor or councilors to which it was entitled on the basis of population. Accordingly, each successive council had from two hundred and fifty to five hundred new and inexperienced members. Not desire or fitness but pure chance determined its personnel. Every section, interest, and class of Attica — if we exclude young men between eighteen and thirty — was adequately represented in it. There was, therefore, a general presumption that it would take the same view of public questions as the ecclesia; that it would do a disservice to its own members should it foster their temporary rights as councilors at the expense of their lifelong rights as members of the ecclesia; that it would, in other words, labor to the best of its ability to present to the ecclesia a well-considered and sufficiently inclusive programme of business. Otherwise, the heliæa had to be faced at the end of the twelve months.

A committee of five hundred impresses us as little less unwieldy than an assembly of five thousand. Clisthenes was of the same opinion. Hence he divided his council into ten sections, or prytanies, of fifty members each, and arranged that each prytany should act for the whole for thirty-six days in an order determined by lot at the latest possible moment. The prytany was constituted in such a way that it was a miniature of the council, just as the council was a miniature of the ecclesia. The lot, again applied at the latest possible moment, determined, furthermore, which of its fifty members should be its chairman, and be present with one third of his colleagues in the council chamber for the single twenty-four hours for which he served. The same man was chairman of the council at its daily session, and he also presided at the ecclesia, should a meeting of the citizens be held on his day of office. A chance nomination for a single day's service, at a time not previously known, was, Clisthenes thought, a sufficient safeguard of council and ecclesia against successful scheming, conspiracy, collusion, or other interference with the popular will on the part of the chairman. He was mistaken; and the later democracy took the further precaution of requiring the chairman to relinquish the presidency at the meetings of the council and ecclesia to a board of nine men chosen by lot for that specific purpose from the non-officiating prytanies of the council. One of the nine, designated likewise by lot, was given the special honor and responsibility of putting the motions and declaring the votes.

Only proposals which originated in a council thus organized came before the ecclesia; but there they might be discussed *ad libitum*, emended, accepted, rejected,

or referred back to the council; and it was even possible
during their consideration to substitute for the resolution of the council an entirely different bill, or to move
that the council bring in a proposition at the next meeting on an altogether irrelevant matter. It was the
deliberate intention of the Athenians that the ecclesia
should consider everything it wanted to consider.

The management of civil administration, subject
to the constant direction of the ecclesia and the watchful supervision of the council, — which in this matter
also acted for the body of which it was a miniature, —
was entrusted to a multitude of committees, each composed normally of ten members. Aristotle, in his
Constitution of the Athenians, specifies the duties of
twenty-five such committees and estimates at seven
hundred the number of citizens engaged annually in
domestic administration. The work of each committee
was definitely circumscribed by law and formed a small
bundle of routine matters. The committees may be
thought of as standing drawn up in a long line for the
council to inspect. Had they been placed one behind
the other in files, the rear committee being responsible
to the one before it and so on down to the front, the
council would have come into direct contact only with
a few powerful committees. Such committees, however,
must have proved impossible for inexperienced councilors to manage. Besides, while the councilors, as agents
of the ecclesia, and subject to its commands, might

properly hold all the civil magistrates to a monthly accounting, it was not thought in accord with democracy that one group of citizens who happened to hold one civil office should have under their direction another group of citizens also engaged temporarily on public work. Though all the committees were thus on the same plane, and recognized only the council as their common superintendent, the work that they did was by no means of equal dignity or importance. It ranged all the way from managing the scavengers to managing the Great Dionysia.

All committees were reconstituted annually. No man could be a member of the same committee twice in his lifetime. At the end of his year each magistrate was required to render an indescribably minute accounting of his public acts, first to specially appointed auditing committees, and finally to the heliæa. It was an easy matter to get an office in Athens, but a very difficult task to get honorably rid of it. For the lot was used to select the requisite number of members for each committee from among the citizens thirty years old or older who had not disqualified themselves by earlier service. The theory that one citizen was as competent as another for public office was thus put into practice. Every office was refilled annually by a chance group of new and necessarily inexperienced men.

While defining constitutions Aristotle lays down the condition for a thoroughgoing democracy that all citizens should hold governmental positions in turn. On this theory, there should have been an approximate agreement between the number of places in Athens and the number of citizens reaching their thirtieth year annually. That, however, was not the case. Even if we assume that men were councilors only once and held only one magistracy in their lifetime, we need to include some of the seven hundred (?) imperial posts in our calculation, and regard them, too, as subject to the conditions of tenure assumed for domestic positions, in order to reach the required total of about thirteen hundred. This is, naturally, an unwarranted and unworkable series of assumptions. It is, however, reasonable to suppose that the majority of Athenian citizens, and practically all of those who made a habit of attending the meetings of the ecclesia held a *deme*, or municipal, position, let us say, in their youth; a post in the council or in the domestic or imperial administration in their maturity; and a place in the register of the six thousand jurors in their advancing years. Recall, now, that three hundred and sixty of the five hundred councilors had to preside at meetings of fifty and five hundred men, and, if chance willed, at one of from five to fifty thousand also; observe that magistrates had not only to know the duties of their office, — which included the reception and preparation of some kind of cases for submission to a panel of jurors, over which they had, moreover, to preside, — but had also to keep accounts which they must defend in a law court; reflect that jury service involved acting as judge and jury in both domestic and imperial litigation, and it will appear that the knowledge of reading and writing which Clisthenes presupposed in all citizens would not have carried a man far in the age of Pericles; he must then have had a working knowledge of parliamentary forms, he must have had the view of administration which comes of being on the inside of the wicket; he must have been so conversant with the law and legal procedure that he could assume heavy personal responsibility for the legality of all bills proposed by him and could argue his own cases when acting as plaintiff or defendant in a law suit. It was a proverb in Athens that "office will show the man." We may be sure that most men took some pains in advance that it did not show them wholly incompetent. It must have left them with a new insight into public affairs. It is fair to say that, as a consequence of all this, the normal town meeting of the Athenians was, from one point of view, an assembly of experts, while viewed differently it possessed simply a high level of amateur attainment, comparable, perhaps, with that Mr. H. G. Wells postulates in his socialistic Utopia.

The office assigned by Pericles to this assembly of high-class amateurs was to choose the best among divergent policies proposed to it by citizens of exceptional endowment. The ecclesia by no means closed the door in the face of such real experts as it possessed. Thus it did not leave it to the council to draw up the specifications for the construction of the naval arsenals or any similarly technical job, but it could and did delegate such tasks to men of special competence. Nor was it so doctrinaire as to entrust the command of its expeditions or the conduct of its diplomacy to chance persons; but it both elected its generals, reëlected them as often as it cared to, and gave them special rights of calling and canceling meetings of the ecclesia and of laying proposals directly before them. It was, accordingly, aware of the difficulty and danger which it faced in settling questions of foreign policy, where the elements involved, being the resources, aims, sentiments, and traditions of other states, far transcended the knowledge of the common citizen; and where error might mean irreparable disaster; where, in fact, error *did* mean irreparable disaster.

The surest way to avoid error was to pick out a single individual of high character, intelligence, and competence, and give him cordial and resolute support in the policy he advocated. The ecclesia was accordingly a great "contest," or *agon*, of statesmen. The Athenians believed in competition. A public contest, in which excellence might be displayed and determined, was arranged to encourage effort in every conceivable employment. To digress a little, there was a contest of potters, as we learn from a gravestone on which an unknown affirms by a mighty oath that he was adjudged the first of all the potters of Attica. There were probably contests of painters and sculptors as well. There were contests of horse-breeders — the chariot- and running-races; contests of athletes of all ages in all kinds of physical exercises, of torch-racers on foot and on horseback; there were contests between the successive prytanies of the council, between detachments of cavalry, and between regiments of foot; at each of many festivals there were contests in singing of five choruses of boys and five choruses of men, each fifty voices strong, so that a single festival called for the training of five hundred singers annually and the production of ten new musical compositions; there were contests of rhapsodists in reciting Homer, contests of rhetoricians; above all contests of tragedians and contests of comedians, each tragic contest demanding twelve new plays annually and the participation of one hundred and eighty choral singers and dancers, each comic contest involving six new plays yearly and one hundred and forty-four choral singers and dancers. The rivalry which produces Olympic records and superdreadnaughts nowadays, the Athenians turned to advantage in art and music as well: with the result that the taste and skill of the artisan as well as the sculptor and painter, of the consumer as well as the producer, became well-nigh faultless; that in the hundred years of the empire close to two thousand plays of picked quality

were written and staged in Athens, while during the
same time from five to six thousand new musical compositions were made and presented. It is estimated that
upwards of two thousand Athenians had to memorize
the words and practice the music and dance figures of a
lyric or dramatic chorus every year. Hence, a normal
Athenian audience must have been composed in large
part of ex-performers, a fact which students of Sophocles
and Aristophanes would do well to bear constantly in
mind.

The reward of victory in an athletic or musical contest was the glory and the prize. Great, indeed, was the
reward which the victor in the supreme contest, the
struggle for political leadership in the ecclesia, obtained.
The man to whom the Athenians gave their confidence
became stronger than a king. "In form," says Thucydides, "their government was a democracy: in reality
it was the rule of their ablest citizen." The man who
was vanquished in a chariot-race might be the victor on
the next occasion. Not so the victim of a decisive
political defeat. His fate was ostracism. That is to
say, he was exiled without dishonor or loss of property
for ten years. The way was thereby cleared for the
victor. By this strange device the Athenians saved
themselves for over two generations from the procras-
tination and uncertainty of distracted counsels. It was
ostracism which made possible the uncrowned kingship
of Themistocles, Cimon, and Pericles; and when, after

the death of Pericles in 429 B.C., this institution failed them utterly, the Athenians were pulled this way and that by rival leaders; till finally, misled by Alcibiades and Cleophon, they were convicted by disaster of being *un*sound judges of *foreign* policy.

There is nothing that dies so hard as a well-nurtured delusion. In the romantic-idealizing view of the Greeks which was long current, the Athenians found leisure for art, literature, and philosophy by having all their work done for them by their slaves.[1] By this means, too, they were enabled to devote themselves freely to politics. If this were so, the inference of Calhoun was a sound one, that seen "in its true light" slavery was "the most safe and stable basis for free institutions in the world." The "first lie" is that the Athenians of the great age, whose dominant characteristic was their vibrant mental and physical activity, were in any sense men of leisure. The few among them who had slaves and other property to the extent of great wealth had to make and manage their own investments. The majority of the farmers had to till the land with their own hands. Many citizens — at least one third of the whole, in all probability — had to earn their living by selling their labor. This they could do easily in the time of the empire. For during that period of rapid commercial and

[1] See particularly Ed. Meyer, *Die Sklaverei im Altertum* (*Kleine Schriften*, pp. 169 *ff.*).

industrial expansion the demand for labor was so great
that the price could be regulated only by the constant
import of slaves and by a steady stream of immigration
from less prosperous parts of Greece. Outside labor
served the purpose in Athens which immigrant labor
serves in the United States to-day. With its growth
grew the need that the material prosperity which occasioned it should endure. The problem of food-supply
became progressively acute and the control of the sea
was soon seen to be an economic necessity. More than
one half of the grain sold on the Athenian market came
ultimately from abroad, as did an even larger proportion of the raw materials of Athenian industry. "The
Athenians are the only people in the Hellenic and barbarian world," wrote an Athenian aristocrat[1] in about
420 B.C., "who are able to control an abundant supply
of raw materials. For if a state is rich in timber for shipbuilding, where will it find a market for it if not with the
masters of the sea? If another abounds in iron or bronze
or linen yarn, where will it find a market except with
the sea-lord? Yet this is the stock from which ships are
made in Athens. One city yields timber to her, another
iron, a third bronze, a fourth linen yarn, a fifth wax,
and so on. Moreover, Athens prevents her rivals from
transporting goods to other countries than Attica by
the threat of driving them from the sea altogether."

---

[1] Pseudo-Xenophon, *State of the Athenians*, II, 10. (The translation used
here and elsewhere, with a few modifications, is that of Dakyns.)

The demands put upon the time of Athenian citizens by the state were enormous, but not such as to cripple economic production. A comparison with modern conditions will make this clear. A little less frequently than once a week the ecclesia met, but the attendance was generally less than one tenth of those qualified. That represents a suspension of work roughly equivalent to our Saturday afternoons and legal holidays. A little oftener than once a week a contest or other public festival occurred, and to these there was, it seems, a pretty general resort. They correspond to our fair-days and Sundays. Preparation for the contests was, perhaps, not more destructive of money-earning time than are our collegiate and university courses. During their nineteenth and twentieth years young Athenians of the upper third trained for the army; but it was not till a century after Pericles's death that universal military service for a similar period was made compulsory—as in modern Europe. We may assume that at least two years of every citizen's life was required for deliberative and administrative work; and, having regard to the imperial service, we may, perhaps, advance this requirement to three. That is an enormous enlargement of modern demands. The same ratio would give the United States two million and a half or three million public employees, exclusive of postmasters and postal clerks, tax-collectors, and day laborers of every description. But a bald comparison of this sort is misleading.

Athens regularly employed a committee of ten to do one man's work, with the result that all of them were free to give nine tenths of their time to their private business. The council during the year and the jury courts at its expiry were there to insure the state that, even if his colleagues would let him, any particular official did not neglect his public duties. Nor was the Athenian practice wildly extravagant so long as the magistrate received, not a living salary, but an indemnity equal only to a common workman's daily wage. The Athenians employed four hundred or even two thousand jurors where we employ twelve; but they had neither high salaried judges nor exacting lawyers to pay, since the judicial system worked without either. The juryman's fee, moreover, was a meagre indemnity, comparable to the old-age pension paid in the progressive countries of modern Europe.

The payment of indemnities for service in the council, the magistracies, the jury courts, and for attendance in the theatre, music-hall, and stadion, was a Periclean innovation. He did not intend to create a class of salaried officials; nor yet to make an advance toward communism. His ideal was political, not economic, equality — to enable all, irrespective of wealth or station, to use the opportunities and face the obligations which democracy brought in its train. Like all the great democratic leaders who preceded him, he was a nobleman by birth and breeding, and, like them, he did not doubt for a moment that the culture which ennobled the life of his class would dignify and uplift that of the masses also. To give the workingman the political insight and knowledge of the Eupatrids; to lend to him the grace and elasticity of movement which physical culture gave them; to fill his memory with the noble thoughts set in melodious and stirring words which they got from their intimacy with great poetry; to inspire in him, though a mere artisan, an artist's taste and fervor for formal beauty — that was to bless him with more than leisure. It was to unite the whole people in a community of high ideas and emotions. It was to make them a nation of noblemen. We do not wonder much that in the furtherance of this cause the men of large wealth in Athens volunteered to assume in turn financial and personal responsibility for the support of the theatre, the opera-house, the stadion, and the gymnasia. It was a heavy burden, but, in the absence of a regular property or income tax, generosity became at once a duty and a wise precaution.

A nation of noblemen is a luxury for which somebody has to pay. Athens, in Pericles's memorable phrase, was "the school of Hellas." It was right, he thought, that the Hellenes should sacrifice something for their education. He had tried to make them all contributory allies of Athens, but had failed in the attempt. As a good schoolmaster he was determined, none the less, to hold those "well in hand" whom he had under his care.

The physical means to this end was the control of the sea. The advantages of sea power in warfare, in enabling the holder of it to circumscribe according to his convenience the area of military action, as well as in facilitating mobilization, transport, and communications, were not perceived for the first time by the English Admiralty, much less by Clausewitz and Captain Mahan. They are stated in the clearest terms by a contemporary of Pericles.[1] Here is what he says: "The subjects of a power which is dominant by land have it open to them to form contingents from several small states and to muster in force to battle. But with the subjects of a naval power it is different. As far as they are groups of islands (and the whole world, we may remark in passing, is now simply a magnified Ægean Archipelago) it is impossible for their states to meet together for united action, for the sea lies between them, and the dominant power is master of the sea. And even if it were possible for them to assemble in some single island unobserved, they would only do so to perish of famine. And as to the states subject to Athens which are not islanders, but situated on the continent, the larger are held in check by need and the small ones absolutely by fear, since there is no state in existence which does not depend upon imports and exports and

[1] Pseudo-Xenophon, *State of the Athenians*, ii, 2 *ff.*

these she will forfeit, if she does not lend a willing ear to those who are masters of the sea. In the next place, a power dominant by sea can do certain things which a land power is debarred from doing; as, for instance, ravage the territory of a superior, since it is always possible to coast along to some point, where either there is no hostile force to deal with or merely a small body; and in case of an advance in force on the part of the enemy they can take to their ships and sail away. Such a performance is attended by less difficulty than that experienced by the army marching along the seaboard to the rescue. Again, it is open to a power so dominating by sea to leave its own territory and sail off on as long a voyage as you please. Whereas the land power cannot place more than a few days' journey between itself and its own territory, for marches are slow affairs; and it is not possible for an army on the march to have food supplies to last for any great length of time. Such an army must either march through friendly territory or it must force a way by victory in battle. The voyager meanwhile has it in his power to disembark at any point where he finds himself in superior force; or, at the worst, to coast by until he reaches either a friendly district or an enemy too weak to resist. Again, those diseases to which the fruits of the earth are liable as visitations from heaven fall severely on a land power, but are scarcely felt by the naval power, for such sicknesses do not visit the whole earth everywhere at once. . . .

There is just one thing which the Athenians lack. Supposing they were the inhabitants of an island, and were still, as now, rulers of the sea, they would have had it in their power to work whatever mischief they liked and suffer no evil in return."

At all costs Athens must retain control of the sea. That meant to keep the fleet constantly in fighting trim. In the effort the Athenians made the most heroic financial and personal sacrifices, demonstrating clearly that popular government need not be self-indulgent. Neither the aristocracy in England nor Napoleon in France was as hard a taskmaster of the people as the majority which ruled in Athens. Between 410 and 402 B.C. — a time of great economic distress — a well-to-do citizen was called upon to expend twenty thousand franks — which are perhaps equal in purchasing power to as many dollars — on what we may call national education and entertainment. His taxes on the account of the fleet amounted in the same years to double as much, or forty-three thousand franks. Great as was the burden of the rich, that of the commons was conceded by their adversaries to have been still greater. "In the first place," writes an aristocrat in about 420 B.C.,[1] "it is only just that the poorer classes and the 'people' of Athens should have the advantage over the men of birth and wealth, seeing that it is the people who man the fleet and put round the city her girdle of power. The steersman, the

---

[1] Pseudo-Xenophon, *State of the Athenians*, I, 2.

boatswain, the lieutenant, the look-out-man at the prow, the shipwright — these are the people who engird the city with power far rather than her heavy infantry and men of birth and quality." Plutarch[1] tells us that on a peace footing Athens kept a fleet of sixty ships on the sea for eight months of every year. To man such a squadron 10,200 rowers, 480 officers, and 600 marines would be required. In other words, one quarter of all the citizens of Athens would have lived on their battle-ships for three quarters of every year. We might believe this report, if it were not contradicted by Aristotle, who in a place, where exaggeration, not reduction, is sus-pected,[2] makes the fleet of Athens, which was constantly in service in time of war, consist only of twenty guard-ships. Hence one twelfth and not one quarter of all the Athenians were on active naval duty during the sailing season of almost every year. In addition, two thousand men were drafted yearly by lot to serve in garrisons throughout the empire; so that, if these are added to the seven hundred (?) imperial magistrates, and the five hundred guards of the arsenals, nearly another one twelfth of the citizens was involved.

This computation takes no account of the demands of naval warfare. In the Athenian dockyards lay ready for action four hundred battleships, from which the requisite number was selected for each particular expedition. If two hundred and fifty vessels were mobilized, as

---

[1] Plut., *Pericles*, XI, 4. [2] *Const. of the Athenians*, 24, 3.

occasionally happened, nearly fifty thousand additional sailors were required. With the use of every possible citizen Athens could not produce such a number. She commonly did her utmost and called upon the allies for the rest.

It is true that tribute was collected from the allies to enable Athens to build the ships and pay the sailors; but it is also true that, in addition, huge sums were contributed for mobilization expenses by rich Athenians and were advanced for heavy war expenses by the Athenian treasury. And Athens gave freely not only of her money but also of her blood. The death roll of one of the ten corps into which the Athenians were divided for army and navy purposes is extant for the year 459 B.C. "Of the Erechtheid *phyle*," it runs, "these are they who died in the war, in Cyprus, in Egypt, in Phœnicia, at Halieis, in Ægina, at Megara, in the same year";[1] and one hundred and seventy-two names follow. It was not the year of a great battle, or of an Athenian disaster, yet in it the death rate must have been nearly twice as great as the birth rate; so costly in lives was the empire to its lords in war-time.

On three specific points and on one general ground, contemporaries both within and without Athens assailed the treatment accorded by the Periclean democracy to its subjects. In no instance, however, is the

[1] Bury, J. B., *A History of Greece* (1900), p. 355.

charge of misbehavior established conclusively, though in this matter, as in so many others in the history of Greece, our judgment is dependent upon the point at which we transfer our sympathy from the city-states, which were the bearers of culture in the Greek Middle Ages, to the whole people, for whose progress and independence urban particularism was finally fatal. "Surely Hellas is insulted with a dire insult," declared the opponents of Pericles,[1] "and manifestly subjected to tyranny when she sees that, with her own enforced contributions for the war, we are gilding and bedizening our city, which, for all the world like a wanton woman, adds to her wardrobe precious stones and costly statues and temples worth their millions." To this accusation the proper retort was, not that having provided adequate protection against Persia, Athens was free to spend the money contributed by the subjects in any way she pleased; for the logical inference was then that the contributions were excessive. Pericles may not have cared to be logical, but he could not ignore forms. Had he been able to show, as has been claimed recently, that he used for building purposes only the sixtieth of the tribute, which had been dedicated as the first fruits to Athena, he would never have been attacked at all. Evidently, he spent on Athenian public works much larger sums derived indirectly from the tribute, for which course the defense actually made seems to have been that the

[1] Plut., *Pericles*, 12. (Translated by Perrin.)

money was due Athens for losses sustained during the invasion of Xerxes and for sums advanced to the war fund during the continuance of the struggle with Persia. In any case the tribute paid was a mere bagatelle as compared with what the subjects saved through having no fleets of their own to maintain.

The charge is more serious that in order to enjoy " the steady receipt of salaries throughout the year derived from the court fees"; to "manage the affairs of the subjects while seated at home without the expense of naval expeditions"; to "preserve the partisans of democracy and ruin its opponents"; to boost the business of hotel keepers and such ilk in Athens, and to win for the common citizens the flattery and consideration that would be shown otherwise only to generals and ambassadors, the Athenians "compelled the allies to voyage to Athens in order to have their cases tried." For it seems clear that the law courts at Athens were usually so clogged with litigation that the gain in having a model code of law and in escaping the fierce partisanship of the local tribunals was largely neutralized by the added expense and humiliation. The real justification of the practice was that it obviated the necessity of sending out naval expeditions.

In the third place Athens took from the allies lands and settled them with impecunious Athenians; but in payment therefor reductions of tribute were given. On the other hand, thousands from the allied cities migrated

to Athens, and, while not escaping military or financial
service, or obtaining Athenian citizenship, they were
cordially welcomed, and enjoyed to the full the commercial and industrial advantages of the metropolis. Again,
Athenians often found it less profitable to invest capital
in Attic land, which was exposed to hostile attack, than
in lands on the islands of the empire, which the fleet protected. Hence there were many Attic farmers in the
subject territory, their right to own foreign real estate
being secured by commercial treaties. There was accordingly economic give and take, the military preponder-
ance of Athens being, however, responsible for the result
that the Athenians abroad were often policemen, the
allies in Athens, hostages.

In all three instances of alleged misbehavior, it must
be admitted that the defense offered by the Athenian
apologists simply added insult to injury in the view of
a majority of the subjects. But for them Athens, arrogant or conciliatory, malefactor or benefactor, was always a foreign governor to be gotten rid of at any cost.
Such uncompromising sentiments time alone could alter,
and to secure the benefits of time Pericles endeavored to
avoid an Hellenic war. His policy of peace after 446 B.C.
was, therefore, the sound policy of an imperialist.

The general ground on which contemporaries criticized the Athenian régime was that under it every assistance was given by the state to the least cultivated
portion of the inhabitants both of Athens and of its

four hundred and twenty subject cities, at the expense of the most intelligent and cultivated elements; that the highest goal of endeavor was moral and intellectual mediocrity. There may be some truth in this contention. The case would be more conclusive, however, if the tendency of the critics to identify intelligence with wealth and cultivation with birth were less obvious. If the point be granted, we must accept the opinion of those historians who affirm that Athens was great in this age despite, and not because of, its democracy. Personally, I do not believe that this was so. I cannot admit that extirpation of the best was practiced in an age in which ideas were created and forms were perfected for their literary and artistic expression which have been the wonder and despair of the men of the highest cultivation from that day to this. Does it not seem like irony that a régime is charged with promoting mediocrity under which rose Sophocles, Herodotus, Phidias, Pericles, Euripides, Hippocrates, Socrates, and Thucydides? Much more important than the leveling tendency of the democracy was the facility it afforded for men of ability both to rise to the top and to find there a sympathetic and critical audience. So much for democracy.

The empire stands approved by the fact that the sharpest accusation now made against the democracy is that it failed to make the empire enduring. On this point the last word — unless it be that no political order has ever been enduring, and that those which have lasted

the longest have been generally of the least worth —
was said by Thucydides [1] over twenty-three hundred
years ago, and I present in conclusion his masterly
account of the circumstances which led to the downfall
of the Athenian Empire: —

"During the peace while Pericles was at the head of
affairs he ruled with prudence; under his guidance
Athens was safe, and reached the height of her greatness
in his time. When the war began, he showed that here,
too, he had formed a true estimate of the Athenian power.
He survived the commencement of hostilities two years
and six months; and, after his death, his foresight was
even better appreciated than during his life. For he had
told the Athenians that if they would be patient and
would attend to their navy, and not seek to enlarge
their dominions while the war was going on, nor imperil
the existence of the city, they would be victorious; but
they did all that he told them not to do, and in matters
which seemingly had nothing to do with the war, from
motives of private ambition and private interest they
adopted a policy which had disastrous effects in respect
both of themselves and of their allies; their measures,
had they been successful, would have brought honor and
profit only to individuals, and, when unsuccessful, crip-
pled the city in the conduct of the war. The reason of
the difference was that he, deriving authority from his
capacity and acknowledged worth, being also a man of

[1] Thucy., II, 65, 5 *ff*.

transparent integrity, was able to control the multitude
in a free spirit; he led them rather than was led by them;
for, not seeking power by dishonest arts, he had no need
to say pleasant things, but, on the strength of his own
high character, could venture to oppose and even to
anger them. When he saw them unseasonably elated
and arrogant, his words humbled and awed them; and
when they were depressed by groundless fears, he sought
to reanimate their confidence. Thus Athens, though still
in name a democracy, was in fact ruled by her greatest
citizen. But his successors were more on an equality
with one another, and, each struggling to be first himself, they were ready to sacrifice the whole conduct of
affairs to the whims of the people. Such weakness in a
great and imperial city led to many errors, of which the
greatest was the Sicilian expedition; not that the Athenians miscalculated their enemy's power, but they themselves, instead of consulting for the interests of the
expedition which they had sent out, were occupied in
intriguing against one another for the leadership of the
democracy, and not only grew remiss in the management
of the army, but became embroiled, for the first time,
in civil strife. And yet, after they had lost in the Sicilian
expedition the greater part of their fleet and army, and
were distracted by revolution at home, still they held
out three years not only against their former enemies,
but against the Sicilians who had combined with them,
and against most of their own allies who had risen in

revolt. Even when Cyrus, the son of the King, joined in the war and supplied the Peloponnesian fleet with money, they continued to resist, and were at last overthrown, not by their enemies, but by themselves and their own internal dissensions."

A summarization such as this, in style austere and authoritative, in content the product of penetrating insight and wonderful sense for political realities, not only bears witness to the greatness of Thucydides; when it is contrasted with similar analyses in Plato and Aristotle it testifies to the loss of power for sustained historical thinking which Greece suffered when men of genius were no longer enriched by the experience which came through living in a state like the imperial democracy of Athens. Not the least of its merits is its self-restraint. Having concluded that the reckless rivalries of her would-be leaders and the reckless dissensions of her citizens ruined Athens, he refrains from assigning a cause for the spirit of lawlessness. It is not Thucydides, but Alcibiades, who declared that democracy was "manifest folly"; not he, but Cleon, who reiterated that "a democracy cannot manage an empire." Thucydides does not despair of democracy. In the case of Athens it was less the unsoundness of the "majority" than the selfishness of the "remnant" that caused the nation to perish. For the demoralization of their leaders, however, the Athenians themselves held Socrates responsible, meaning to incriminate the Sophistic movement. Who shall say that they were wrong? And who shall hold democracy responsible for the evils of the Sophistic movement?

SELECT BIBLIOGRAPHY

1. WILAMOWITZ-MOELLENDORFF, ULRICH VON. *Von des attischen Reiches Herrlichkeit* (1877). In *Reden und Vorträge*, pp. 27 *ff*.
2. JEBB, R. C. *The Age of Pericles* (1889). In *Essays and Addresses*, pp. 104 *ff*.
3. MEYER, EDUARD. *Geschichte des Altertums*, IV (1901).
4. WILAMOWITZ-MOELLENDORFF, ULRICH VON. *Staat und Gesellschaft der Griechen* (1910): C. *Die athenische Demokratie*, pp. 95 *ff*.
5. ZIMMERN, ALFRED. *The Greek Commonwealth* (1911).
6. CAVAIGNAC, E. *Histoire de l'Antiquité*, II: *Athènes* (480–330), (1912).

III

FROM SPARTA TO ARISTOTLE

A CURIOUS legend about the Spartans arose in the age that followed the conquest of Persia by Alexander the Great. It was then reported that they were the kinsmen of the Jews. According to one version of the story, Judæa was founded by a Spartan named Judæus, who had accompanied the god Dionysus from Thebes on his triumphal progress through Asia. According to another account, the Spartans were descendants of Abraham, the strongest of the children of Israel having migrated to Greece at the time Moses led the remainder out of Egypt to the land of Canaan.[1]

This absurd legend, of which the Greek origin is unmistakable, seems to have been responsible for a certain *rapprochement* between the two peoples. Despite the first book of the Maccabees, which affirms the contrary, it is, indeed, impossible that Areus I, king of Sparta between 308 and 264 B.C., wrote to Onias I, Jewish high priest, demanding and offering a community of goods, and that Jonathan Maccabæus, one hundred and fifty years afterwards, sent greetings to the Spartans, together with the word that the Jews "at all

[1] Schürer, *Geschichte des jüdischen Volkes im Zeitalter Jesu Christi*, I [3] (1901), pp. 236 *f.* See notes.

times without ceasing both in their feasts and other convenient days remembered them in the sacrifices which
they offered, and in their prayers, as reason was, and
as it becameth them to think upon their brethren." [1]
Nothing is more unlikely than that the Spartans volunteered to divide their "cattle" and property with the
Jews only a short time before they crushed with great
bloodshed a communistic movement among their own
citizens, unless it be the thought that the prayers and
offerings of the Jews went up continually to Jehovah for
the prosperity of heathen who were also backsliders.
Nevertheless, that communications were actually established between the Judæa of Onias and Jonathan and
the Sparta of Areus and Menalcidas, we cannot doubt;
and, indeed, we have still other evidences that the alleged
community of origin was turned to account by the Jews.
There was evidently a considerable Jewish settlement in
Sparta.

When we seek to discover the reason for this strange
conjunction of the warrior community by the Eurotas
and the religious community by the Jordan, we are
helped by observing that in another Hellenistic legend
the Jews are made the kinsmen of the gymnosophists, or
naked philosophers, of India. The Greek mind was at
this time fascinated by the great problem of subordinat-
ing the species of things to their proper genera, of perceiving the types by means of which individual objects

[1] 1 Macc. XII, 11.

became intelligible parts of a cosmos. It was the age of Aristotle and Theophrastus, Menander and the New Comedy, of idealistic portraiture. Hence the temptation was irresistible to bring into family relationship the various societies of men in which the principle of caste dominated; to regard it as unessential that in Judæa the people were there to support the priests, in Laconia to support the soldiers, in India to support the Brahmans. In each case there was found an odd community, in which, so far at least as the state could accomplish it, all human interests were subordinated to one, be it war and preparation for war, religious practices of a ritualistic character, or theosophical speculation.

Had the Greeks known it, there was a further analogy of an external sort between the Spartans and the Jews which they would have delighted to establish. For at about the same time that a richly diversified national life was narrowed down in Judæa to a single interest under the stress of complete preoccupation with the means of regaining Jehovah's favor for his chosen people, Sparta ruthlessly compressed and crushed a many-sided and progressive culture to the end that her citizens might become trained soldiers, having but one esprit, the esprit de corps of a professional army.

Prior to 580 B.C. Sparta was the home of poets and musicians. It was for a chorus of Spartan maidens, the élite of the noble families, that Alcman wrote the exquisite lines on the breathless calm of nature which Goethe has

made familiar to all lovers of poetry. In hollow Lacedæmon — a valley rich with vegetation suggestive of boun-
tiful harvests, down which the steel-gray Eurotas runs,
swift and turbulent, over its rocky bottom, and over
which rise on either side the snow-capped ridges of
Taygetus and Parnon, their slopes resonant with the
songs of the nightingales in the mating season — in this
secluded spot, whose haunting beauty is a joy forever to
all who have seen it, there was reared a famous temple
of Athena, "Athena of the Brazen House," at a time
when in Athens itself the city's protecting goddess had
to be content with a crude, primitive sanctuary.

All this, and much besides, was observed, and the
proper inferences drawn, by Eduard Meyer twenty
years ago;[1] so that the amazement with which the
English archæologists, who have excavated in Laconia
during the past five or six years, report their remarkable
"finds" is a source of no little amusement to the wary.
They have discovered that prior to 580 B.C. Sparta was
the maker of a kind of artistic pottery which was known
and imitated in far-distant Cyrene and Tarentum; that
she then had trade relations with Egypt and Lydia;
that "combs, toilet-boxes, elaborate pins and bronze
ornaments, seals, necklaces, and gold and ivory gew-
gaws" were made and used — witnesses *for* "a golden
age of Spartan art," *against* the puritanical spirit tra-
ditionally attributed to early and middle Sparta.[2]

[1] *Geschichte des Altertums*, II[1] (1893), pp. 562 *f.*
[2] Dickins, *Journal of Hellenic Studies*, XXXII (1912), p. 12.

In Athens, as we have seen, supremacy in art and literature was attained by making universal among citizens the spirit and culture of the aristocracy, the whole people, thus ennobled, being supported on the shoulders of the tributary allies and enriched by the commercial advantages of maritime empire. The development of Sparta was directly the reverse of this. There the aristocracy, whose exuberance of life and responsiveness to sensuous impressions are attested with sufficient certainty, was destroyed in the sixth century B.C.

This century was one of repression in Greece generally; whence some historians have called it the epoch of the Greek Reformation. It is the time of the "Seven Wise Men," from one of whom came the Delphian motto "nothing in excess," a time in which the riotous joy of living and the fresh spontaneity of the so-called Ionian Renascence were subdued by a force, which might have been everywhere a blight, — as in Sparta, — but which in fact, when later the inspiration of the great Persian War came, exerted the gentle restraint which marks the classic in Greek art and letters. In this perilous period the aristocracy of Sparta perished, and with it the ideals and accomplishments of which it had been the exponent.

The instrument of repression of all that was superior to the average in Spartan life was the college of the five ephors, which Cicero compares with the tribunate in Rome. The ephors acquired such power that they made the continuance of even the kingship dependent upon the submission of the kings to their authority; and upon the kings, as upon all others, they enforced the new rules of law of which they were the living expositors.

The development of Sparta, like the development of Rome, from aristocratic to republican government is characterized by the absence of tyrants. The fact is that the tribunate in the one case and the ephorate in the other was tyranny in commission, the division of its powers between ten and five annually changing officers respectively having proved to be a sufficient safeguard against the concentration of executive power in the person of a single individual, be he an inherited king robbed of monarchical rights or an ambitious demagogue aiming at their restoration.

The new rules of law which the ephors enforced prescribed in minute detail the life of the citizen from the moment of his birth to the time of his death. They were the regulations of a military school in which war alone was taught, of military barracks when war was already declared. From seven years of age to sixty the entire energies of the male half of the population were directed toward being prepared for war. Boys and men drilled and hunted, learned to use their weapons and campaigned, danced and exercised, ate in the "messes" year in and year out, and never escaped the watchful eyes of trainers, subalterns, officers, and ephors.

No one in Sparta had to make his own way in life. His whole course was mapped out for him before he was born. No citizen had any business cares; for all trade and industry were tabooed, and the lands which he inherited he could not sell. Neither could he buy those of another. The agricultural laborers were serfs, the sullen and recalcitrant Helots, of whom there were fifteen to every Spartan; the clothing and weapons were made by the contented and tractable Periœcs, who outnumbered the Spartans five to one, and formed with their one hundred hamlets and their contiguous territories an insulating band round Helots and Spartans alike. Iron money was the only local currency, though silver had, of course, to be given in payment for the articles which were imported from abroad. These, however, were reduced to a minimum, and such foreigners as made their way through the wall of Periœcs were rounded up at intervals and forcefully expelled.

All the pretty things of their earlier life, the Spartans chose to do without. Coarse fare and unlovely houses, piazzas devoid of statues and inclosed in unsightly and flimsy public buildings; no theatres, no new music, no new ideas of any kind; mothers who gave up their little children and their grown sons without flinching; wives who violated fundamental instincts that their offspring might be more perfect; homeless boys who went half-naked winter and summer, slept in pens in the open air like cattle and got their food and living by their wits;

girls who would hardly have known their brothers, brides who would hardly have recognized their husbands, mothers who would hardly have been able to distinguish their own sons, were it not that there were less than five thousand brothers, husbands, and sons in all — of such was the new Sparta, to whose citizens the ephors issued the annual command "to shave their mustaches and obey the laws." Long-haired and tangly-bearded, in groups of about fifteen each, they lounged and ate and slept in the three hundred tents, or barracks, which lined Hyacinth Street. There they kept their long spears and their armor.[1] Thence, clad in their scarlet cloaks, they issued in time of danger or of war to take their places, group by group, in the five carefully drilled regiments of which the Spartan phalanx was composed. Quietly, at an appointed hour in a single night, the whole army might steal away without confusion, trailing after it, on occasion, thirty-five thousand Helots to attend to the commissariat. Five thousand Periœc hoplites might follow at its heels, and with machine-like precision, to the sound of flutes played in the austere Dorian mode, ten thousand Lacedæmonian soldiers might advance into battle against foemen who were always comparatively ill-organized, and who often fled before a single blow was struck.

The secret of this strange perversion of the natural life of man is to be found in the declaration of war

[1] Schoemann-Lipsius, *Griechische Alterthümer*,⁴ 1 (1897), pp. 261 *ff.*

annually made by the ephors upon the Helots. They
could not follow it up by a campaign waged in regular
fashion; for that would have been to destroy their own
serfs. But they picked out young soldiers, and sent
them about among the Helots, with instructions to
strike down secretly all who seemed restless or over-
ambitious. The chief centre of Helot disaffection, at
least in the seventh and sixth centuries B.C., was on the
far side of Mount Taygetus, in Messenia. There the
yoke of serfdom chafed more than elsewhere, not least
because those whose estates the Helots of Messenia
tilled for one half the yield lived beyond the snow-
capped ridge which shuts in that country on the east.
The Messenians aspired to regain their lost independence. The Helots of the Eurotas Valley had no such
ambition. They were, therefore, slower to revolt against
injustice; but their aim, when an insurrection *did* come,
could be nothing less than the extermination of their
masters, or at least an exchange of position with them.
Moreover, their very proximity to the five villages
which constituted the unwalled city of Sparta, and the
very weight of their numbers made the Spartans live
in ever-present fear of a massacre. Constant prepared-
ness for war was, accordingly, a simple mandate of self-
preservation.

The Spartans thought it unwise that any of their serf-
tilled estates should lie in or outside the ring of Periœc

land. It would not do to have fuses, so to speak, of Helots running through the wall to the outside world, or to have masses of Helots beyond the wall, exposed directly to foreign manipulation. Hence the formation of the Periœc ring set definite limits to the territory of Sparta. It could be enlarged in but one way — the widening of the ring by the reduction of more and more outlying states to the status of Periœcs. And it was in this way that the Spartan dominions were in fact enlarged in the seventh century B.C.[1]

At the end of this century, however, Sparta came into conflict with cities which, unlike the mountain and maritime hamlets situated roundabout Laconia and Messenia, were too strong and high-spirited to submit to Spartan control. They had, therefore, to be treated leniently, since Sparta could not crush them altogether and would not leave them alone. And the reasons for conciliatory action were strengthened by the fact that Sparta had now to act abroad with a sharp eye to the possibility of a servile insurrection at home. There was never anything mechanical or idealistic in the foreign policy of the ephors. Hence, first with Tegea at about 560 B.C., and thereafter with all the states in the Peloponnesus, excepting Argos and Achæa, Sparta concluded a treaty, the imperialistic aspect of which was that they agreed individually to accept Sparta's leader-

[1] See particularly Niese, *op. cit.* in Select Bibliography at end of chapter.

ship in all defensive wars and in offensive wars to which they had assented.

The Peloponnesian league, thus formed, stood for the autonomy and freedom of its members; but Sparta, by championing aristocracies against tyrants and democracies, and using to its own advantage the jealousies of its allies as well as their fears of outside powers, dominated it for one hundred and eighty years, and made it during all that time the main steadying influence in Greek politics. Twice it was enlarged into an Hellenic league, first during the three years of the great Persian invasion (480–478 B.C.), and again for ten years after the dissolution of the Athenian empire (405–395 B.C.). On the earlier occasion, the ephors felt relieved of an intolerable burden when in 477 B.C. the Ægean cities, over four hundred and twenty in number, abandoned Spartan for Athenian leadership. And in the forty-six years that followed, not they but the Athenians were the aggressors. During that epoch of democratic fervor,[1] it was an uphill struggle for the champions of aristocracy to maintain their position; and the war of political principles was even carried into Sparta, when, in 464 B.C., the Helots of Messenia made a last desperate fight for their liberty. The Spartans profited, however, during the last third of the fifth century B.C., by the discredit into which democracy came among cultivated people through the mistakes and excesses of Athens;

[1] Beloch, *Griechische Geschichte*, I (1893), pp. 439 *ff.*

and at the end of the Peloponnesian War they were again able to make the Peloponnesian league an Hellenic league by incorporating into it Athens and the Ægean cities which they had just "liberated" from Athenian tyranny.

A successful war may strengthen a nation, but not when victory lays upon it a task that is beyond its powers to perform. Such would have been the case had Athens won at Syracuse. Such was the issue of Ægospotami. This we can readily see by examining briefly, first the situation in Sparta, and then the position of Sparta in Hellas, during the existence of her second Hellenic league.

The Spartans of military age now numbered only about two thousand. War had done its part in reducing them to this handful. Close intermarriage had done even more. In the case of large families, the subdivision of lots which then occurred impoverished sons so greatly that they could no longer stand the expense of the military clubs, upon membership in which, however, citizenship depended. So far did the evil implicit in this condition go that brothers refused to divide their inheritance, and possessed not only one house, but one wife in common. Men could neither buy land nor sell it, but they might acquire it by marriage or by gift; and since the rich, then as always, tended to marry among themselves, property, and with it citizenship, remained eventually in the possession of a very few. Much of the land, which was the only wealth, came into the hands of women. A plutocracy thus developed in Sparta as the number of the Spartans diminished; and in this way the domestic situation became still further ominous by the growth in the city of a considerable body of disfranchised and discontented "inferiors" and half-breeds.

The perils which attended this situation are revealed by the following incident as described by Xenophon in his *Hellenica:* [1] —

"Now Agesilaus (401–360 B.C.) had not been seated on the throne one year when, as he sacrificed one of the appointed sacrifices in behalf of the city, the soothsayer warned him, saying: 'The gods reveal a conspiracy of the most fearful character'; and when the king sacrificed a second time, he said: 'The aspect of the victims is now even yet more terrible'; but when he had sacrificed for the third time, the soothsayer exclaimed: 'O Agesilaus, the sign is given to me, even as though we were in the very midst of the enemy.' Thereupon they sacrificed to the deities who avert evil and work salvation, and so barely obtained good omens, and ceased sacrificing. Nor had five days elapsed after the sacrifices were ended, ere one came bringing information to the ephors of a conspiracy, and named Cinadon as the ringleader; a young man robust of body as of soul, but not one of the peers. Accordingly, the ephors questioned their informant: 'How say you the occurrence is to take place?' and

[1] III, 3, 4 *ff.*

he who gave the information answered: 'Cinadon took me to the limit of the market-place, and bade me count how many Spartans there were in the market-place; and I counted—king, and ephors, and elders, and others, maybe forty. *But tell me, Cinadon*, I said to him, *why have you bidden me count them?* and he answered me: *Those men, I would have you know, are your sworn foes; and all those others, more than four thousand, congregated there are your natural allies.* Then he took and showed me in the streets, here one and there two of our enemies, as we chanced to come across them, and all the rest our natural allies; and so again running through the list of Spartans to be found in the country districts, he still kept harping on that string: *Look you, on each estate one foeman — the master — and all the rest allies!*' The ephors asked: 'How many do you reckon are in the secret of the matter?' The informant answered: 'On that point also he gave me to understand that there were by no means many in their secret who were prime movers of the affair, but those few to be depended on; *and to make up*, said he, *we ourselves are in their secret, all the rest of them — Helots, enfranchised, inferiors, Periœcs, one and all. Note their demeanor when Spartans chance to be the topic of their talk. None of them can conceal the delight it would give him if he might eat up every Spartan raw.*' Then, as the inquiry went on, the question came: 'And where did they propose to find arms?' The answer followed: 'He explained that those of us, of course, who are enrolled in regiments have arms of our own already, and as for the mass — he led the way to the war foundry, and showed me scores and scores of knives, of swords, of spits, hatchets, and axes, and reaping hooks. *Anything or everything, he told me, which men use to delve in the earth, cut timber, or quarry stone, would serve our purpose; nay, the instruments used for other arts would in nine cases out of ten furnish weapons enough and to spare, especially in dealing with unarmed antagonists.'* Once more being asked what time the affair was to come off, he replied his orders were *not to leave the city.*"

The ephors, wishing to remove Cinadon from Sparta without suspicion, sent him on a mission to Aulon. He was to arrest certain persons, and among them "a woman, the fashionable beauty of the place — supposed to be the arch-corruptress of all Lacedæmonians, young and old, who visited Aulon." His escort seized him instead and wrested from him the names of his accomplices. "His fate was to be taken out forthwith in irons, just as he was, and to be placed with his two hands and his neck in the collar, and so under scourge and goad to be driven, himself and his accomplices, round the city. Thus upon the heads of those," concludes the pious Xenophon, "was visited the penalty of their offense."

Beset with dangers such as this, the Spartans had to tread warily. They drafted Periœcs into their army so as to make it about fifty-six hundred strong. They picked

out Helots, trained and emancipated them, and used
them abroad as soldiers. They took mercenaries into
their service and distributed them according to local
needs under Spartan captains, acting always, however,
on requests from local governments. They got large contingents of troops from their old allies, whom, however,
they left free of tribute, financing their government with
a thousand talents raised annually from the former allies
of Athens. With the funds thus secured they hired
rowers and marines for the warships which their allies
furnished and thus patrolled the sea as well as the land.
They got a moral mandate for empire by upholding
everywhere aristocracy, real or sham, against democracy, and by assuming the rôle of champion of Greece
against the barbarians. This did not prevent them,
however, from forming an alliance with Dionysius I,[1]
who had just made himself tyrant of Syracuse, or from
working in harmony with Persia as long as that was
possible.

"The growth of Lacedæmon," said Timolaus of Corinth[2] in 394 B.C., "seems to me just like that of some
mighty river — at its sources small and easily crossed,
but as it further and further advances, other rivers dis-
charge themselves into its channel, and its stream grows

---

[1] The successive tyrannies in Syracuse and the empires of Syracuse over
the West Greeks have been omitted of necessity in this book. They have
been examined with particular care by Freeman in his *History of Sicily* and
with particular sympathy by Beloch in his *Griechische Geschichte*.

[2] Xenophon, *Hellenica*, IV, 2, 11 *ff.*

ever more formidable. So it is with the Lacedæmonians. Take them at the starting-point and they are but a single community, but as they advance and attach city after city they grow more numerous and more resistless. I observe that when people wish to take wasps' nests — if they try to capture the creatures on the wing, they are liable to be attacked by half the hive; whereas, if they apply fire to them ere they leave their homes, they will master them without scathe themselves. On this principle, I think it best to bring about the battle within the hive itself, or, short of that, as close to Lacedæmon as possible."

The advice was sound; but the wasps could not be caught at home. It was not till Athens had beaten the Spartans at sea, and Thebes had beaten them on land, that Epaminondas reached the hive. He then broke up the Peloponnesian league, emancipated the Helots of Messenia, and substituted, for the once considerable power which had saved the Peloponnesus from serious attack for two hundred years, a multitude of little city-states such as existed elsewhere in Greece — rather, such as came to exist elsewhere in European Greece, when, a few years later, with Epaminondas's death, the supremacy of Thebes ceased, Athens was abandoned by the states which had joined her against Sparta, and the empire of Dionysius I in the west dissolved, shortly after his death, into its constituent parts.

Theoretically, conditions should then have been ideal.

In the case of the Greeks the deep-seated human instinct to compare the present disadvantageously with the past was not checked by a theory of evolution conceived as progress, such as misleads many sensible people nowadays to imagine that the farther back they go the more rudimentary political and social conditions become. The golden age of the Greeks lay in "the dark backward and abysm of time." In early days, before the rise of the Spartan and Athenian empires, every city, so it was believed, had "lived in peace, free and autonomous, and in secure possession of its own territory." For more than a century men had struggled to bring back those blessed times, and now at length their efforts, it might have seemed, had been crowned with success. Every city in Greece, great and small, had apparently regained its liberty and autonomy.

At the same time men had made a persistent effort to reëstablish in each city "the constitution of the fathers," and under the Spartan hegemony the favorable opportunity for success in this campaign had seemingly come. But it then appeared that, apart from the general understanding that citizenship was to be reserved to those who could afford to pay taxes and provide themselves with the arms and knowledge of arms necessary for fighting, no two persons agreed as to what the "ancestral constitution" was. It proved to be in reality the ideal of each reformer and each politician, and since the age was one in which most of the ordinary restraints were lacking as they seldom are in the history of civilized man, the transition from an unpopular ideal to a conspiracy was apt to be singularly abrupt. The outcome of the attempts to restore the urban particularism of mediæval Greece and the constitutions of the over-praised olden time was unsatisfactory to everybody. Barren wars of city against city instead of large enterprises directed by imperial ambitions; an atmosphere murky with plots and counter-plots, where once there had blown the strong wind of steady civic progress; and, in addition, national disaster and humiliation despite manifest military superiority — these were the bitter fruits of political reaction in Greece during the Spartan supremacy.

It was in this unhappy age that the science of government was born, and it bears its birthmark to the present day. The midwife, to use his own homely figure, was Socrates, whom the Athenians, tarred on by Aristophanes, put to death "for corrupting the youth and introducing strange gods." He, of course, denied the accusations, and claimed that he deserved the honors of a public benefactor for taking men individually and showing to them how ill they understood the virtues on which all societies are based, to wit, justice, wisdom, temperance, and courage. No one, he thought, could make them better citizens except by promoting truth and dispelling ignorance about these things. His execution consecrated his mission. It was the sowing of dragon's teeth from which sprang up armed warriors, of whom the most doughty were Plato and Aristotle.

The vice of the Socratic school was a noble one — an enormous overestimate of the value of education. "Truth is the beginning of every good thing," says Plato,[1] "both to gods and men; and he who would be blessed and happy, should be from the first a partaker of the truth, that he may live a true man as long as possible, for then he can be trusted; but he is not to be trusted who loves voluntary falsehood and he who loves involuntary falsehood is a fool." There was, of course, only one truth; which, being discovered, should be taught; which, being taught, must be acted upon, since, if men really knew what was right, it was impossible, Plato thought—ignoring the frailty or obstinacy of the human will— that they should not do it. "Discover the truth." "Teach it." These are the two Socratic commandments.

I have no intention to make an exposition of the political philosophy of Plato and Aristotle,[2] but to do something much more modest: to explain wherein and wherefore they missed the truth in the matter of Greek imperialism, and to notice some of the historic forces which they disregarded. If I deal with the *Laws* rather than the *Republic* of Plato, it is because it is his more mature and less imaginative work.

[1] *Laws*, v, p. 730. (The translation used here and elsewhere in the book is that of Jowett.)
[2] For what is here omitted see the excellent little book by von Arnim, *Die politischen Theorien des Altertums.*

It was upon his immediate present that Plato focused his attention; to the analysis of its political and moral strength and weakness that he turned his penetrating intelligence; for its betterment that he wrote and taught and suffered. The past he peopled with creations of his own exuberant fancy, of popular misconception, of defective knowledge. He can be easily convicted of gross historical errors. And what is more serious; he has no real regard for historical truth and no sense whatever for the real factors in historical developments. Without the slightest qualm of conscience, and without taking the least pains to ascertain the facts, Plato alters the divine and profane history of his people to make it serve his purpose. And he does this on principle: "The legislator,' he says,[1] "has only to reflect and find out what belief will be of the greatest public advantage, and then use all his efforts to make the whole community utter one and the same word in their songs and tales and discourses all their life long." To disagreeable things in the sacred story he gives a short shrift. Since the gods are perfect, every report that tends to tarnish the lustre of their reputation must be false. The history of mankind is solved by a similar formula; since justice is the *sine qua non* of public and private prosperity and happiness, all reports which affirm the conjunction of injustice with well-being, or of righteousness with misfortune, need correction or suppression.[2] History, accordingly, be-

[1] *Laws*, II, p. 664.   [2] *Laws*, II, p. 662.

comes a happy hunting-ground for edifying stories. It at once ceases to yield lessons, which, being grounded in the realities of human experience, are less apropos, perhaps, than the political theorist may like, but are alone valuable.

Plato's absorption in the present led him to misread not only the past, but also the future. For the false standard with which he measured past policies and institutions is not less characteristic than the false judgment which he formed of the drift of contemporary events. The future belonged, not, as he dreamed, to the autonomous, archaizing city-state, but to the movement for their unification which he condemned. He tried to mend city constitutions when the world required the creation of larger territorial states. He watched with attention domestic politics when foreign politics were chiefly worth watching.

A glance at the ideal state portrayed by Plato in the *Laws* [1] shows in what sense he read his history. His citizens are to have "their food and clothing provided for them in moderation," the latter through "entrusting the practice of the arts to others," the former through getting from the land, which slaves till for a part of the produce, "a return sufficient for men living temperately." They are to have "common tables in which the men are placed apart, and near them are the common tables of their families, of their daughters and mothers, which,

[1] VII, p. 806.

day by day, the officers, male and female, are to inspect."
They are not, however, to live fattening like beasts; for
"such a life is neither just nor honorable, nor can he who
lives it fail of meeting his due; and the due reward of the
idle fatted beast is that he should be torn to pieces by
some other valiant beast whose fatness is worn down by
brave deeds and toil."

Naturally, Plato does not wish his ideal citizens to
meet such an ignominious end. He proceeds to prescribe
a régime for them in which, after a most carefully nur-
tured childhood, three years are spent on reading and
writing, three more on learning to play the lyre, and
others still on the study of arithmetic, geometry, astron-
omy, and law, and on the practice of dancing, wrestling,
running, hunting, and many kinds of military exercises.
The citizens to be protected from fatty degeneration in
this way are, it should be observed, the women as well as
the men.

The children's stories are prescribed and are unalter-
able; so are the music and the dancing and the poetry.
The law studied is that of the commonwealth, with which
every citizen is to be inoculated. The moral and religious
ideas are to be fixed, and death is the penalty set for
heterodoxy. Everything is to be made and kept rigid,
the number of the houses, of the farms, of the citizens, of
the children, of traders, artisans, and foreigners, the
maximum and minimum wealth of everybody. In other
words, the community which Plato in his old age pro-

posed as a model is not a thorough-going communism, like that of his more youthful and more famous *Republic*. It is simply a system of governmental control carried to its logical extreme — an emended and perfected edition of Sparta.

That a well-born Athenian, disgusted at the license which resulted from letting people live as they pleased, should have planned to put all citizens in an administrative strait-jacket, is not surprising. Many of us to-day object to a "wide-open town." But that Plato, whose practice in discussion was "to follow the argument whithersoever it might lead," should have idealized a state in which freedom of thought and freedom of speech were denied altogether, shows (even if we make all allowances for the idea, that, if things were perfect and there was but one perfection, all changes must be harmful) how unreal and involved in self-contradiction was the thinking of the best Greeks in this age of reaction.

The theory of individual liberty, as applied in Athens, had led, in the economic sphere, thought Plato, to the exploitation of the poor by the rich, and, in the political sphere, to the exploitation of the rich by the poor. Plato, therefore, discarded the theory of individual liberty altogether. He was dominated by a general view of life in which all the natural human instincts and cravings were harmful. The only hope for states was that they should educate their best citizens to be their governors. Plato, accordingly, nailed to the mast the doctrine of salvation by education, and despaired of all states in which the carefully trained few of high intellectual capacity did not make the laws and enforce them. Of all these ideas the Athenian democracy was the negation, and Plato hated it with the bitterness of a passionate nature.

That Plato hated the Periclean democracy as a political system is also intelligible from his hatred of imperialism upon which it was based; and there are those to-day, who, for the same reason and also because of a mistaken notion of its dependence upon slavery, find Athenian democracy justified, if at all, by its fruits; who contemplate its art and literature with the same mingled feelings with which they view the hectic beauty of the consumptive. Plato is not of their company. The fruits he finds even more deleterious than the stock which bore them. "In music," he writes,[1] meaning thereby poetry interpreted by the voice with musical accompaniment, — "in music it was that there first arose the universal conceit of omniscience and general lawlessness; — freedom came following afterwards, and men, fancying that they knew what they did not know, had no longer any fear, and the absence of fear begets shamelessness. For what is this shamelessness, which is so evil a thing, but the insolent refusal to regard the opinion of the better by reason of an over-daring sort of liberty?" Whereto the Spartan who is his interlocutor says: "Very true."

[1] *Laws*, III, p.700. The same initial cause of degeneracy is postulated in Plato's *Republic*, VIII, p. 546.

"Consequent upon this freedom," continues the speaker, "comes the other freedom, of disobedience to rulers; and then the attempt to escape the control and exhortation of father, mother, elders, and when near the end, the control of the laws also; and at the very end there is the contempt of oaths and pledges, and no regard at all for the gods, — herein they exhibit and imitate the old so-called Titanic nature, and come to the same point as the Titans when they rebelled against God, leading a life of endless evils."

The modern critic, even if he endorses the sharp indictment of Euripides, the poet of the most radical democracy, — that he destroyed the character of Attic tragedy by introducing into it elements from melodrama and the operatic concert, by perverting the grand style of its text and music by vulgar flippancies and incongruous measures, by substituting for artistic development of characters and plot disturbing discussions of the woman question and the latest sensations in philosophy and science, by turning the ancient gods and heroes into burlesque through having them argue and act like contemporary sycophants and sophists, — the modern critic, even Professor Shorey,[1] for example, in his spirited defense of the Sophoclean drama, would abandon Plato, I fancy, when he makes the drama the fundamental cause for the decline of Athenian greatness.

In his *Laws*, Plato is dealing with what, chastened by

[1] *Greek Literature* (The Columbia University Press, 1912), p. 11.

age and experience, he regarded as correctible things. The lust for private possessions, for land and home, wife and children, he once placed in this category, but he does so no longer; and in other respects he makes wide concessions to human frailties. With greed for wealth, however, he concluded no truce. It is Greeks, mark you, of whom Plato[1] says: "Love of wealth wholly absorbs men, and never for a moment allows them to think of anything but their own private possessions; on this the soul of every citizen hangs suspended, and can attend to nothing but his daily gain. Mankind are ready to learn any branch of knowledge, and to follow any pursuit which tends to this end, and they laugh at every other. . . . From an insatiate love of gold and silver, every man will stoop to any art or contrivance, seemly or unseemly, in the hope of becoming rich; and will make no objection to performing any action, holy or unholy and utterly base, if only like a beast he have the power of eating and drinking all kinds of things, and procuring for himself in every sort of way the gratifications of his lusts."

Such were the evil conditions of the present when one citizen despoiled his fellow and every city its neighbor. It had been different in the past. Before the introduction of luxurious tastes to stimulate inventions and of coined money to destroy a sense for the natural limits of wealth, men had "worked in summer, commonly, stripped and barefoot,[2] but in winter substantially

---

[1] *Laws*, VIII, p. 831. [2] *Republic*, II, p. 372 b.

clothed and shod. They fed on barley-meal and flour
of wheat, baking and kneading them, making noble
cakes and loaves; these they served up on a mat of reeds
or on clean leaves, themselves reclining the while upon
beds strewn with yew or myrtle. And they and their
children feasted, drinking of the wine which they had
made, wearing garlands on their heads, and hymning
the praises of the gods, in happy converse with one
another. They took care that their families did not
exceed their means: having an eye to poverty or war."
But it was not to an age of such rude simplicity that
Plato would recall his contemporaries. He would,
indeed, restore the virtues which existed among the
early country folk before the rise of modern cities and
the establishment of the capitalistic régime; but, while
hostile to transmarine commerce, retail trade, industries,
banking, interest, and all other accompaniments of
interchange between cities, which he regarded as generally undesirable and provocative of wars and conquests, he imagines his ideal people in possession of city
culture and the articles of luxury and convenience
secured through the capitalistic organization. His citizens are, indeed, farmers, but they are gentlemen
farmers, who have their money invested in land and
slaves and live on their dividends, free to devote their
leisure to athletic, intellectual, and other worthy pursuits. They will be free from greed of wealth because
they all possess a competency, which Plato defines as

---

enough to live "temperately," Aristotle as enough to live "with liberality and temperance." Neither philosopher thinks of poverty except as the ordainer of body- and soul-destroying work, work which degrades those who have to perform it, and makes slavery their natural condition. Plato and Aristotle would make all tillers of the soil and workers at the trades and crafts slaves and aliens. They were to exist simply to provide the conditions of "good living" for their masters or superiors; whereupon "we must not conceal from ourselves," says Aristotle,[1] "that a country as large as the Babylonian or some other of boundless extent will be required if it is to support five thousand citizens in idleness." Even in America, where, to use the current formula, ten per cent of the people own ninety per cent of the wealth, the economic situation proposed as ideal by the most enlightened reformers of the fourth century B.C. has hardly been reached. Whether Plato failed to realize that he was condemning nine tenths of people to perpetual bondage and ignorance; or, realizing it, refused to think of anything but the perfection of the few, the conclusion is alike inevitable: he had failed miserably to trace to their historical causes both the cultural barrenness of Sparta and the astounding fertility of his own Athens.

[1] *Politics*, II, 3 (6), 3, p. 1265 *a*. (The translation used here and elsewhere in the book is that of Welldon: the text that of Immisch.)

Had Aristotle lived in the commonwealth of Plato's *Laws*, he must have suffered the same fate that Socrates suffered in Athens. For, though far from ungrateful to his teacher, he was not a docile pupil. By birth he was a Stagirite, by experience a citizen of the world. He did not, like Plato, form his youthful impressions in a milieu that was poisoned with bitterness at a demoralized democracy. The Athens to which he came as a lad of seventeen was still a democracy, and a very unhealthy one at that, and for it he had little liking; but his was a more dispassionate nature than was Plato's. He was not a great historian.[1] *That* the discovery in Egypt in 1890 of one of his many lost historical works has proven clearly; but he was a very learned man, and perhaps came to as close a comprehension of earlier Greek history as was possible for a political philosopher who had nothing to guide him but the unscientific methods then in vogue for investigating the past.

By its very nature science is objective. It is not inhuman, but it is deliberately impersonal. In this respect it contrasts sharply with the arts. The greatest artist may be the man who embodies in his verse or stone or colors moods and thoughts which must be in "widest commonalty spread," but which constitute in the aggregate his own self or soul. History is of course a science, but not one of the common type. Unlike the ordinary scientist, the scientific historian has to practice, not

[1] Bury, J. B., *The Ancient Greek Historians*, pp. 182 *ff*.

self-suppression, but self-expansion. He must become conscious, so far as that is possible, of the prejudices and special interests of his own age, and, divested of them, he must migrate into a strange land in order to bring back thence a report that is at once an unbiased account of what he has seen and a story that is comprehensible to his fellow-citizens, or, at least, to his fellow-historians. He dare not treat the past as one in spirit with the present, or as resolvable into precisely the same factors. He must be alive to the existence of many different pasts leading to the present in no pre-determinable succession, much less progression. The points must make a line, but the line may be of any conceivable curve. Aristotle was far from arriving at a full appreciation of the difficulties of historical inquiry; but, unlike Plato, he took infinite pains to acquire historical knowledge.

He did not idealize the constitutions of the olden times. Since all men then carried daggers, the presumption, he says, is that they needed them and used them. Since conditions where violence reigned must have continued indefinitely, if political change had been prohibited, he finds it good as well as inevitable that laws be modified from time to time. The permanency of those of Sparta is worthy of high praise; but he traces the corruption and decay of the Spartan state to failure to make needed reforms. In general he strikes a much more just balance between Spartan and Athenian achievement than does Plato.

The first test he applies to institutions, such as the family and the state, is their naturalness — their source in the nature of man as that is revealed in his history. He was well aware that a political science that was based upon *perfected* human nature was, indeed, suited only for "gods and sons of gods"; that the only principles of government which had real value were those which had approved themselves in practice. "All discoveries," he says, [1] "have been already made, although in some cases they have not been combined, and in others, when made, are not acted upon." "The *Politics* of Aristotle," says a recent writer, "is the one great book on the science of government because it is the only one which is wholly empirical."

That is too high praise. For the *Politics* of Aristotle differs from the *Prince* of Machiavelli in other respects, of course, but noticeably in that the Greek has moral ideals, the Italian none. With Aristotle, as with Plato, the state has an ethical purpose. He requires it to justify not only its acts but its existence. Iniquitous governments might exist, — Aristotle's world was full of them, in fact, — and his mind was too curious of all things political for him to leave them out of his observation: he has, indeed, considered minutely the ways and means for the preservation of all kinds of states, and has shown therein that he had as keen an eye for the realities as had Machiavelli himself. But he would

[1] *Politics*, II, 2 (5), 10, p. 1264 *a*.

never have permitted, much less advised, his legislator
to use foul means to establish a just government or fair
means to establish an unjust one.

On the establishment of governments, moreover, he
spends very little thought. This, however, is with
Machiavelli the main matter, as he himself says near
the opening of the second part of his work: "The chief
foundations of all states, new as well as old or composite,
are good laws and good arms; and as there cannot be
good laws where the state is not well armed, it follows
that when they are well armed they have good laws.
I shall leave the laws out of the discussion and shall
speak of the arms." Had the Greek heard him he would
have scoffed at both the argument and the conclusion.
The argument is, of course, sophistical, and the conclusion saved only by the fact that Machiavelli had
already considered the political weapons with which
rulers should operate. The *Politics* is a handbook for
legislators; the *Prince* a set of instructions for potentates.
For the latter the ways and means of *acquiring* power
was, in Machiavelli's judgment, the all-important
thing; whereas the legislator's possession of power is
taken for granted by Aristotle, and it is assumed throughout his entire treatment that, if the lawgiver knows the
constitution, the laws, and the system of education which
are best adapted to the economic, social, and political
conditions of his state, he can at once introduce them.

In a measure, therefore, the *Prince* and the *Politics*

supplement each other, though Aristotle would have
been horrified at the idea. For in his thinking, in anything approximating to an ideal world, each city was
free to order its internal affairs as it thought best, and,
having this liberty, if it was shown what was best, it
must, according to the Socratic psychology, immediately adopt it; whereas — to give the devil his due —
Machiavelli was actuated, in formulating his precepts
for Prince Lorenzo, by the vision of a united Italy,
the realization of which by his pupil was to wash away
the crimes committed in subjecting to his will the city-
states of the peninsula. The conquest of Italy was,
accordingly, the goal of the ideal Prince's endeavor;
whereas, though Aristotle in one passage of the *Politics*[1]
notes that "if the Greeks were united in a single polity
they would be capable of universal empire," he regards
such a union as highly undesirable. To him a state that
was not a city was a rudimentary and very imperfect
state. It ceased to be a state at all when it ceased to be
free. Hence a city could have subjects, that is to say,
slaves, but not dependencies. And since in his thinking
it was natural inferiority alone that justified slavery,
and this was found especially among the nations of
Asia, and not at all in Greece, no Greek city could rightly
enslave the inhabitants of any other Greek city: it could
wage war and organize slave raids only against barbarians.

[1] VII (IV), 6 (7), I, p. 1327 *b*.

The birthmark which we have noted on Plato is an inheritance from unreasoning hatred of democracy. That which mars above all the political thinking of Aristotle comes from the aversion instinctively felt by his age for imperialism. That this, too, is a disfigurement, we may show in a few concluding remarks. "It is necessary," says Aristotle[1] in concluding his plea that a mixed constitution is best for the common run of states, "it is necessary to begin by assuming a principle of general application, viz., that the part of the state which desires the continuance of the polity ought to be stronger than that which does not"; and he proceeds to point out that "strength" consists neither in numbers, nor property, nor military or political ability alone, but in all of them combined, so that regard has to be taken of "freedom, wealth, culture, and nobility, as well as of mere numerical superiority." Nothing could be more cold and objective than the thinking of Aristotle on this important matter. Yet by an extraordinary oversight he lets "strength" exert a decisive influence *within* the city-states, while he ignores altogether the effect of varying population, wealth, and political and military ability in determining the relations *between* them.

The whole of the political thinking of Aristotle is dominated by the idea that the world of men is made up of an infinite procession of inferiors and superiors, the

[1] *Politics*, IV (VI), 10 (12), 1, p. 1296 *b*.

desire to forge ahead being one of the most fundamental instincts of human beings. If an omniscient God were to arrange the inhabitants of each city in a line according to their real "strength," he would place few of them abreast. No Greek betrays more naïvely than Aristotle does the national consciousness of the Hellenes that they stood at the head of the honor roll of peoples. It was, therefore, imperative upon them to conquer the Asiatics; for he finds it to be a beneficent command of nature, issued primarily for the advantage of the weaker, that superiors should rule inferiors.

Among moral philosophers Aristotle is characterized by his refusal to let himself be led astray by a visionary ideal of human equality. Nevertheless, while recognizing that Greek cities, even more than individuals, differed in "strength," he refused to let the "strong" use their advantage. He sets apart the sphere of interurban, that is to say, international, relations as one in which the "universal principle," that superior rule inferior, shall not apply. In a visionary world, the "strong" man, on Aristotle's theory, is a "gentle" man; but in the real world, he is a ruler. Had Aristotle not been blinded by the prejudices of his age against imperialism, he must have seen the necessity that in the real world the "strong" state would also be the ruler. It is one of the enigmas of history that Aristotle was the contemporary and subject of Philip II of Macedon, one of its ironies that he was the tutor of Alexander the Great.

SELECT BIBLIOGRAPHY

1. SCHÖMANN-LIPSIUS. *Griechische Altertümer,*[4] 1 (1892), pp. 197 *ff.*
2. BURY, J. B. *A History of Greece to the Death of Alexander the Great* (1900).
3. MEYER, EDUARD. *Geschichte des Altertums,* v (1902).
4. NIESE, B. *Neue Beiträge zur Geschichte und Landeskunde Lakedämons: Die lakedämonischen Periöken.* In *Nachrichten der Gött. Gesell. d. Wissenschaften* (1906), pp. 101 *ff.*
5. ARNIM, HANS VON. *Die politischen Theorien des Altertums* (1910).
6. GOMPERZ, TH. *Greek Thinkers,* III (1905), IV (1912).

IV

ALEXANDER THE GREAT AND WORLD MONARCHY

ALEXANDER THE GREAT was born in 356 B.C. His mother, Olympias, was a half-civilized Molossian princess whose fresh beauty, revealed at a wild religious fête on mystic Samothrace, had caught the roving fancy of Philip of Macedon. Their union had the further attraction to Philip that it might bring Epirus under his suzerainty.

Philip wished his wife to be his chief concubine rather than his consort. Olympias, a proud and passionate woman, chafed at her husband's marital infidelities, and had the will and courage to revolt and act for herself when Philip set her aside in 337 B.C. She cannot be acquitted of guilty knowledge of the murder of Philip which occurred a year later at the marriage arranged by him between her daughter and her brother. The act was timed to assure the accession of her son, who was its chief beneficiary.

"My father," Alexander is reported to have said twelve years later to his mutinous Macedonian soldiers,[1] "found you nomadic and poor. Clad in sheepskins, you tended your meagre herds on the mountains, and had to fight grievously for them against the Illyrians, Triballi,

[1] Arrian, *Anabasis*, VII, 9, 2 *ff.*

and Thracians on your borders. He gave you cloaks to wear in place of hides, he led you down from the hills into the plains, he made you the match in battle of the barbarians who dwelt near you; so that you depended for your safety thenceforth, not on the inaccessibility of your country, but on your own valor. He taught you to live in cities; he appointed good laws and customs for your governance. He made you lords, instead of slaves and subjects of those barbarians by whom you and your possessions had long been harried. The greatest part of Thrace he annexed to Macedon. By seizing the most suitable points on the seacoast, he threw open your country to commerce. He gave you the chance to work your mines in safety. The Thessalians, before whom you had cowered, half dead with fright, he taught you to conquer, and by humbling the Phocians he made your road into Greece, hitherto narrow and difficult, broad and easy. To such a degree did he lower the Athenians and the Thebans, who had ever been ready to fall upon Macedon, — and herein had he my help, — that, instead of your paying tribute to Athens and taking orders from Thebes, it was to us in turn that they went for protection. Into the Peloponnesus he passed and set matters to rights there; and, being appointed commander-in-chief of united Greece in its projected war against Persia, he achieved this high distinction, not so much for himself as for the commonwealth of Macedonia."

The words are not those of the great king himself: they are at the best a paraphrase of the ideas expressed by him on the occasion; at the worst they are the free invention of an historian concerned only with having Alexander say what the situation seemed to him to demand. However that may be, they are a good account of the wonderful work which Alexander, as a boy and young man, saw his father accomplish for Macedon. "What a man we had to fight," said Demosthenes,[1] his great enemy. "For the sake of power and dominion he had an eye put out, his shoulder broken, an arm and a leg injured. Whatever limb fortune demanded, that he gave up, so that the remnant of his body might live in glory and honor." "Taking everything into account," says Theopompus,[2] the far from generous contemporary historian of his achievements, "Europe has never produced the like of Philip, the son of Amyntas."

The court of Philip was rough and boorish. Revels, disgraced by drunkenness and debauchery, interrupted the king's wars and amours. In Pella men behaved like Centaurs and Læstrygonians, sneered the fastidious Athenians; and the frenzy which wine inspired in Philip, religion inspired in Olympias. In wild abandon she let herself be possessed with the spirit of the god, Dionysus, and roamed the hills at night in the company of other women equally intoxicated, brandishing the thyrsus and the "wreathèd snake," shouting with

[1] *De Cor.* 67.   [2] Müller, F. H. G., 1, *Frg.* 27.

ecstasy. Hers was the religion which William Vaughn Moody, with poetic license, singled out in the splendid *Prelude* to his *Masque of Judgment* as characteristic of the world into which Christ was born. It was really abhorrent to the best Greek feeling, and was repressed with stern cruelty by Rome.

Passion, fierce and generous, the main source of heroic action, was bred in the bone of Alexander. His imagination, naturally fervent, was fed by tales of his ancestor Achilles which he heard at his mother's knee, and fired by the vistas opened out to it by the exploits of his father. At thirteen Philip gave him Aristotle as his tutor, and during the formative years of his youth he studied poetry with this great teacher. The poetry was Greek, not Macedonian. In it were found the ideals of the people to which Alexander belonged in spirit and in blood, if not in nationality; thence came the ideas tinged with emotion which fasten themselves like barbed arrows in the memory of the learner — the ideas of right and wrong, of heroism and tenderness, of regard for parents and for duties; as Plato would say, of justice, wisdom, temperance, and courage — which color all subsequent thinking and constitute character. The Greeks have still something to teach us as to the educative power of great poetry.

The commandments of Homer, whom Aristotle never ceases to cite in his philosophical works, went over into the flesh and blood of Alexander, and in him Achilles, the youthful hero of the Iliad, became in a real sense incarnate. Next after Homer, Alexander rated and knew the Attic tragedians, the continuators and improvers of Homer, according to Aristotle, who, therefore, bases his *Poetics* largely upon tragedy, as being the highest form of dramatic art.

There can be no question of the influence of Aristotle in determining the literary interest and taste of Alexander. It seems also clear that the young prince came at least to know, and probably to share, his teacher's curiosity as to natural history; for he afterwards sent specimens back from Asia for Aristotle's botanical and zoölogical collections. This being the case, it seems incredible that he should have received from him no instruction in politics; that Aristotle, the pupil of Plato, who had himself gone to Sicily to educate the young Dionysius II for his high place, should have failed to communicate to the future ruler of Macedon and of Greece the ideas which he had formed as to the best kind of government. We can imagine the thousand opportunities which their three years of close association in the country seat at Mieza offered for the discussion of politics: how Aristotle explained that virtue or merit or political capacity, or however the elusive Greek word *arete* be translated, gave the best claim to leadership, and that the best of all forms of government was that in which the man of the highest virtue ruled; "that," to use his own words,[1]

[1] *Politics*, III, 11 (17), 12, p. 1288 *a*.

"wherever there is, as it happens, a whole family or an individual so superior in virtue to all the rest that the virtue of this individual or family exceeds that of all others in the state, in that case it is but just that this family should enjoy a regal or supreme position and that this individual should be king. For ... this is not only in accordance with the principle of justice usually alleged by the founders of polities, whether aristocracies, oligarchies, or democracies, in all of which the claim to rule is dependent on superiority, although the superiority is not the same; but it accords also with the theory we laid down before. For assuredly it is not proper to put to death or outlaw or even ostracize this preëminent individual or to require him to become a subject in his turn. ... The only alternative is that they should yield him obedience, and that he should be supreme, not on the principle of alternation, but absolutely. . . . It will be a wrong," he urged,[1] "to treat him as worthy of mere equality, when he is so vastly superior in virtue and political capacity, for any person so exceptional may well be compared to a deity upon the earth." Again and again, in season and out of season, often doubtless to the annoyance of the impatient young prince, who feared lest his father's victories should leave him nothing to do, Aristotle[2] must have harped on the theme that "man is naturally a city-dwelling animal and that one who is

---

[1] *Politics*, III, 8 (13), 1, p. 1284 *a*.
[2] *Politics*, I, 1 (2), 9, p. 1253 *a*.

not a native of a city, if the cause of his isolation be natural and not accidental, is either a superhuman being or
low in the scale of civilization, as he stands alone like a
'blot' on the backgammon board. The 'clanless, law-
less, hearthless' man so bitterly described by Homer is a
case in point; for he is naturally a native of no city and a
lover of war," We can imagine the philosopher insisting
that just as city life was synonymous with civilized life,
so city was synonymous with state; that the highest of
all human activities, the exercise of political functions,
was destroyed the moment a city became dependent upon
an outside power; that subjects could not exist permanently unless the conquered were natural inferiors like
the Asiatics; that it was, however, to the interest of such
persons that they should be ruled by their superiors, in
the case of Asiatics, by the Greeks. Such were the oft-
repeated maxims of the political philosopher in whose age
Philip rejoiced, it is said,[1] "that his son was born, since
his teaching would make him worthy of his father and
equal to the position to which he was to succeed." Such
was the literary and political education of Alexander:
his military training and his knowledge of affairs he got
in the unrivaled school of his father; but in this connection it is well to remember the admission of Napoleon:[2]
"War is a singular art ; I can assure you that fighting
sixty battles taught me nothing I did not know at the

---

[1] Aulus Gellius, *Noctes Atticæ*, IX.
[2] Johnston, R. M., *The Corsican*, p. 498.

first one. The essential quality of the general is firmness, and that is a gift from heaven."

It is not my purpose to give a biographical sketch of Alexander, nor yet to tell the story of his marvelous conquests, or to estimate the consequences of his work on the later course of history. I have had in mind while preparing this chapter first to emphasize such features in his family and education as help to explain his political thinking, and then, somewhat in Plutarch's fashion, to pick up such incidents in his career as show concretely how precisely he aimed to organize his world empire.

Where the political sagacity of Alexander stood forth most conspicuously, according to Napoleon, was in the skill with which he appealed to the imagination of men. Love of symbolism was ingrained in his nature. By an act which he went deliberately out of his way to perform he contrived again and again to illumine an entire situation, to drive home a lesson, to reveal a policy. In a way it was a kind of advertising; a means of conveying to the world at large in an unmistakable manner the will and attitude of the monarch. But it was more than that. It was the application in the world of politics of a mode of expression with which the Greeks were familiar in the world of the plastic arts.

The first instance of this sort of thing was the destruction of Thebes in 335 B.C. At the accession of Alexander a year earlier, all Greece had seethed with insurrection.

Philip was dead in the full vigor of manhood, and a strip-
ling of twenty was about to take his place. By a prompt
advance southward Alexander nipped the threatened
revolt in the bud; and to secure himself for the future,
he put a garrison in the citadel of Thebes, where the most
manifest disaffection had existed. A few months later,
however, while he was cleansing his northern frontiers,
preparatory to attacking Persia, the Thebans, acting on
the false report that he had fallen in battle, and in conjunction with Athens and other Greek cities, revolted a
second time. With almost incredible secrecy and celerity
Alexander came upon Thebes, took it by assault, sold
the inhabitants into slavery, and razed the city to the
ground. No such disaster had overtaken a Greek city
(outside of unhappy Sicily) since the destruction of
Miletus by the Persians in 493 B.C. It showed beyond
the shadow of a doubt what the Greeks had to expect
if they continued to make trouble while Alexander was
absent in Asia. And on this occasion one object lesson
was contained within another: by sparing the house of
Pindar, the destroyer of Thebes proclaimed his regard
for Hellenic civilization; distinguished himself clearly
from the destroyers of Miletus and other barbarians.

Next year, when about to open his attack on the Persian empire, Alexander sent his army across the Hellespont by the usual route from Sestus to Abydus; but he
himself proceeded to Elaius where he sacrificed at the
tomb of Protesilaus, and prayed that he might have a

better fate than was his who first of Agamemnon's men set foot on the soil of Asia. Then crossing the Hellespont to Harbor of the Achæans, he went up to Ilium where he dedicated his armor to Athena Ilias and took in its place some weapons said to have been used in the Trojan War. After appeasing the *manes* of Priam and entreating them to forgive him, a descendant of Neoptolemus, Priam's slayer, he laid a wreath on the tomb of Achilles, while his bosom friend, Hephæstion, laid another on that of Patroclus. Whereupon he proceeded to rejoin his army. The incident stirred in every Greek a thousand memories. He saw another Agamemnon set out to take another Troy; another champion of the Hellenes in their eternal struggle with the peoples of Asia. In no way could Alexander more clearly identify his undertaking with the long cherished dreams of the whole Greek race. It was the nearest that a ruler of that time could come to proclaiming a holy war.

At Gordium, where Alexander's troops spent their first winter in Asia, there stood on the citadel the cart in which, according to the story, Midas, a peasant's son, had driven to the meeting-place of the Phrygians on the day when unexpectedly he was proclaimed their king. The legend had spread thence around the country that whosoever unfastened the knot of cornel bark which held the yoke to the shaft of this cart would become king of Asia. This task Alexander essayed in vain. Then he drew his sword and cut the thong in two. Thereby he announced both his departure from the policy of Philip, which had been simply to emancipate the Ionian Greeks, and the forthcoming execution of his own policy, which was to take from the Persians their dominion over Asia.

After his first victory at the Granicus River Alexander advanced along the Ægean seaboard as far as Cilicia, securing as he went all the coast towns in Asia Minor which had contributed ships to the Persian fleet. This plan of campaign he adhered to after his second victory at Issus over Darius, when, instead of keeping in touch with his defeated enemy and of following him into the interior, as the ordinary common sense of war commanded, he let the King go, and spent a year in seizing the naval towns between Cilicia and Cyrene. This he did in order to destroy the Persian fleet, an end which he could not otherwise attain, since he had no ships of his own. To leave the enemy's fleet in possession of the Mediterranean, however, while he was campaigning far in the heart of the continent would have been to jeopardize all that he had already accomplished, and, in particular, to leave to the Persians the means of causing a general insurrection among the Greeks, whom he rightly feared more than the Persians. This long détour southward to Egypt is, accordingly, amply explained by sound strategical considerations. That, however, cannot be said of Alexander's sensational march through the Sahara to the oasis of Siwah in the hinterland of Cyrene. There, in mysterious aloofness, lay an oracle of the

Egyptian Ammon whom the Greeks called Zeus. Just as Dodona in Epirus had been eclipsed in times past as an oracular seat by the shrine of Apollo at Delphi, so this in turn had waned in prestige and credit when it became known gradually to the Greeks that Zeus Ammon revealed unfailingly the future to his priests at Siwah. For more than two generations prior to Alexander's visit the Ammonium had been the Mecca of pilgrims, and the recipient of gifts from all parts of the Greek world. Athens had even built a sacred trireme, the so-called "ship of Ammon," to carry public messengers to and from the oracle. In Egypt the Ammon of Siwah was of no account as compared with the Ammon of Thebes; but among the Greeks the Ammon that was known and revered was, to speak with Plato, the Ammon of Cyrene. Alexander knew well the impression which would be produced in the official and pious world of Hellas should the priests of Ammon greet him as the son of their god. This, however, they were bound to do on his arrival at the temple, since to omit this formality would have been to refuse allegiance to the new Pharaoh who had just been recognized in Egypt; for every Pharaoh from time immemorial was officially a son of Ammon. It was the peculiarity of Siwah that the ruler greeted there as the son of Ammon was presented authoritatively to the Greek world as the son of Zeus.

The march across the desert to Ammonium was accomplished only with supernatural assistance, according to the official report; and deliberate mystery shrouded the interview of Alexander with the god. It is with no impropriety, as we shall see presently, that Tennyson brings his fine poem on the great king to a climactic close with an allusion to the occurrence: —

> "High things were spoken there, unhanded down;
> Only they saw thee from the secret shrine
> Returning with hot cheek and kindled eyes."

One thing, however, was stressed in the official version of what happened: the desired greeting was given publicly to Alexander by the eldest of the priests. And its import was enhanced by the arrival of messengers to say that oracles to the same effect had been given simultaneously by the Sibyl of Erythræ and Apollo at Branchidæ, where a long silence of over one hundred and fifty years was interrupted thereby. As to the private interview Alexander wrote to his mother that "secret things were divulged to him which he could communicate only to her personally."

I shall revert to the significance of the visit to Siwah presently. Meanwhile, it will suffice to note that it was quite in character with the methods already adopted by Alexander that he should seek in this bizarre way to impress upon the imagination of men a new idea; to disclose by a sensational action of this kind an important change of policy. And it is paralleled by several incidents in his later career.

Twelve months after leaving Siwah, Alexander was master of Persepolis. This was the capital of Persis, a land of some half a million inhabitants whom Cyrus and Darius had made lords of a subject population not much below that of the Roman empire. For over two hundred years forty millions of people had looked to Persis and Persepolis as the seats of the mighty. The "city of the Persians" and the palace of their kings which it contained were the manifest symbols of empire: the one Alexander gave over to his soldiers to pillage, the other he fired with his own hand, thus proclaiming to the world that the end of a dynasty had come. His own part in this catastrophe — which affected the imaginations of men in some such way as did the capture of Rome by Alaric in 410 A.D. — was taken conspicuously. Starting up from a banquet, he and his companions, among whom was the beautiful Athenian courtesan Thais, went in Dionysiac revel to the sound of flutes through the streets to the palace, and threw the torches which they had taken with them from the feast upon the cedar beams of the roof. Once the flames had shot up and the desired effect had been produced, Alexander ordered the fire to be extinguished.

Early in the following year Alexander entered Ecbatana, the summer capital of the Persian empire, and Darius became a fugitive. Up to this point Alexander had been hegemon of the Hellenic league as well as king of Macedon, and, on liberating the Greek cities in Asia from Persian control, he had added them to the league. Now that the war against Persia, for which the league had been ostensibly formed, had ended, Alexander thought the time had come to relieve himself of the partnership into which, following the policy of Philip, he had entered at the opening of his reign. This he did in his usual dramatic way. He discharged all the Greek troops put under his command by the league, and made elaborate provision for their transport back to the coast and across the Mediterranean to Greece. To every Greek city which had sent him a contingent, its return was a message that Alexander was no longer bound by the treaties made when the league was formed. This did not mean, as he took pains to show, that it was freed thereby from all obligations toward him. Over the Macedonians he ceased at this point to be hegemon, but he still remained their king.[1]

A little later he appeared before his astonished Macedonian officers clad in what pleased him of the costume of the Persians. The tiara and the sleeved jacket and the baggy trousers he did not adopt, but he took their soft undergarments, and, as the symbol of authority, the diadem. He also remodeled his court in the Oriental fashion, adding purple to the uniform of the guards, chamberlains, and, if a dubious report is to be trusted, a harem. Finally in 327 B.C., shortly after his romantic marriage with Roxane, a Persian princess of the Sogdian

[1] See above, page 28, and below, page 243.

nobility, he added the requirement that all who were admitted to his presence should kneel at his feet and kiss the dust before him. "Chares of Mytilene,"[1] who was master of ceremonies when this custom was inaugurated, "says that Alexander, while drinking at a symposium, offered his goblet to one of his comrades, who, taking it, rose and went to the hearth, where, quaffing it off, he first knelt and kissed Alexander's feet, then kissed his cheek and returned to his couch. All present did the same except Callisthenes," who proffered the kiss on the cheek without first kneeling and thus earned the disfavor of the king. With this rather lame conclusion was enacted the prologue of what his old Macedonian nobles regarded as a great tragedy.

"It has been thought," says Eduard Meyer,[2] "that *proskynesis*" — to use the technical term for this ceremony — "was only the natural expression of the fact that by the arbitrament of battle Alexander had become lord of the Persian empire and legitimate successor of Darius. And, indeed, there is truth in this idea. But the meaning of the requirement, and the historical significance of the occurrence and of the conflict which it occasioned, are by no means exhausted when proskynesis is regarded as a harmless concession to the views of his Oriental subjects. The essential point is that Alexander demanded it of the Macedonians and Greeks also. It is precisely in this matter, however, that the views of Orientals and

[1] Plut., *Alex.* 54. [2] *Kleine Schriften*, pp. 314 *ff.*

Europeans collide most squarely and typically. Herein exists an antagonism which is independent altogether of race and nationality. We cannot say how it arose, but it dominates the whole course of the cultural and political development of the regions in question. The Oriental, be he a Semite, an Egyptian, an Indo-European, a China-man, or of any other stock, finds it natural that in inter-course with others he has to humble himself; that he call himself their servant, them his masters; that he kneel in the dust, not only before the king, but before all supe-riors, without lessening thereby the sense of personal pride with which he, too, may be animated.

"To the European, on the other hand, such demeanor involves the destruction of his own personality. Never will a free man call himself the slave of another. Rather, he will always speak of himself in confident tones, with a strong feeling of his own worth. . . . Prostration and kissing the dust are due, in European thinking, only to a god who is thereby acknowledged to be the lord of the worshiper, in whose presence the worshiper can have no will of his own.

"It was among the Greeks, in their free republics, that this feeling developed to its full strength. It finds typical expression in the story of the Spartan heralds, Sperthies and Bulis, who, although they had surrendered themselves to the Persian king to be executed, refused to prostrate themselves before him; 'for in their country,' Herodotus makes them say, 'it was not customary to kiss the dust before a man, nor had they come for that purpose.' The stories of Themistocles who rendered the required homage, and of Conon who on its account avoided an audience with the King altogether, despite the high value it would have had for him, are similarly significant. In demanding proskynesis, accordingly, Alexander offended Greek sentiment violently. Rather, what he thereby demanded was the acknowledgment that officially, in his capacity of king, — his private position is a different matter altogether, — he was no longer a man, but a god."

In other words, when Alexander demanded that Greeks and Macedonians fall at his feet and kiss the dust before him, he demanded that they recognize him as a god, as in fact the son of Zeus. This ceremony had no such implications for the Persians; but, as we shall see in a moment, in Alexander's thinking, the Persians were to cease to exist; they were to be made Hellenes by education.

Alexander set out for Asia with a firm belief in the absolute superiority of Hellenic culture; and in this belief he remained fixed to the end. To establish Hellenic life throughout Asia, he regarded as the main object of his conquests. His Hellenic ideals he revealed to the astonished natives at almost every halting-place on his march; for on such occasions he again and again held gymnastic and musical contests after the Greek pattern. As we have seen, he had learned from Aristotle that city-life and Hellenic life were synonymous, and that without political activity city-life was animal rather than human in character. Accordingly, he displayed a feverish energy in founding Greek city-states everywhere in the conquered territory, but particularly in the regions of the Far East where urban life had been hitherto lacking. Like mushrooms overnight, towns by the scores sprang up behind him on his line of march; so vast was the immigration into Asia from Greece and Macedon even during the thirteen brief years of his reign.

The fact was that by founding cities Alexander lessened enormously his military and administrative difficulties. For every city took from his shoulders responsibility for maintaining order, collecting taxes, and dispensing justice in the territory assigned to it — necessary tasks, now that a European state was arising in Asia, which could be performed otherwise only by the creation of a bureaucratic system of officials. This, however, was a non-Hellenic institution for which Alexander had naturally no liking. In the future he saw the whole world — that of Asia which he had already conquered and that of the Far West which he meant to conquer — honeycombed, like Greece itself, with a multitude of city-states, each a separate cell with a town in its centre, each possessed of a general assembly and a council, magistrates of its own choosing and laws of its own making or adoption, each the home of free men speaking the Greek language, fostering Greek art and letters, and fighting with Greek arms and tactics. It was a grand vision, which failed of realization in Alexander's time and thereafter; but it set forth an ideal toward which future generations moved for over five centuries.

It is clear that Alexander never lost faith in the absolute supremacy of Hellenic culture. Certainly the place of unlimited authority which he reserved for himself above the world of city-states and their law-bound citizens, was the one prescribed for the ideal wise man, the man of supreme political ability, by Aristotle his tutor. That Aristotle thought of a different *pambasileus* for each city-state and Alexander of a single "absolute monarch" for all, is a non-essential difference, and it is simply in the institutions which Alexander found necessary to translate the idea of the philosopher into the world of reality that Hellenic practice and custom were violated.

These outlandish institutions, however, Alexander employed as means for the better dissemination of Greek life and thought, without being conscious, perhaps, that they were destructive of the spirit which they were intended to preserve.

On the other hand, it is indisputable that Alexander revised his tutor's, and his own youthful, opinion as to the worth of the Asiatics. What he came to think of Semites and Egyptians we do not know; and it may be that he continued to regard them as naturally servile

and, hence, condemned them to remain forever hewers
of wood and drawers of water for the Hellenic or Hellenized citizens in whose cities they were to live. But as to
the Medes and Persians and the kindred Iranian stocks
of the Far East, the views of their conqueror changed
radically when he came really to know them, and to
appreciate fully the magnitude of the task which he had
undertaken.

He found that they had spirit and capacity comparable to those of the Greeks and Macedonians themselves.
That they caused him no physical repulsion is shown by
his falling in love with and marrying Roxane. Teach
them the Greek language, draw them along with the
immigrant Greeks into the body politic of the new
cities, equip them with Macedonian weapons, drill them
in the Macedonian fashion, and distribute them in the
Macedonian regiments; above all, use the nobles in the
high administrative posts, and it seemed to Alexander
possible, within a short time, to fuse the new masters of
Asia with the old into a new cosmopolitan race.

With iron resolution he carried this policy forward
despite all opposition. Then, choosing the dramatic
moment of his return to Susa after his Indian campaign,
he arranged an extraordinary marriage as a symbol of
the contemplated fusion of the dominant peoples of
Europe and Asia. "He himself," says Arrian in his
Anabasis,[1] quoting Aristobulus, an eye-witness, "mar-

[1] VII, 4, 4 *ff.*

ried Barsine (rather Stateira), the eldest of the daughters of Darius, and, in addition to her, another, the youngest of the daughters of Ochus (the able predecessor of Darius), Parysatis. Earlier, too, he had wedded Roxane, the daughter of Oxyartes of Bactria. To Hephæstion he gave Drypetis, who, too, was a daughter of Darius and sister of the wife he took himself; for he wished the children of Hephæstion to be cousins of his own children. To Craterus he gave Amastrine, the daughter of Oxyartes, Darius's brother; to Perdiccas, the daughter of Atropates, satrap of Media; to Ptolemy, his aide, and to Eumenes, his private secretary, children of Artabazus, to the one Artacama, to the other, Artonis. To Nearchus he gave the daughter of Barsine and Mentor, to Seleucus the daughter of Spitamenes of Bactria; and in like manner to his other companions he gave the most famous of the daughters of the Medes and Persians, to the number of eighty. The marriages were celebrated in the Persian manner. Seats were placed in order, and on them the bridegrooms reclined"; and at this point we may let Chares, master of ceremonies, interrupt Arrian and describe the setting which he had arranged for the service.

"It was," he says,[1] "a hall of a hundred couches, each large enough for two to recline at table, and in it each couch, made of twenty minas' worth of silver, was

---

[1] Athenaeus, XII, pp. 538 *ff*. (Translated by Wheeler in his *Alexander the Great*, pp. 477 *f*.)

decked as for a wedding. Alexander's had feet of gold.
And to the feast were bidden all his Persian friends, and
given places on the opposite side of the hall from himself
and the other bridegrooms. And all the army and the
sailors and the embassies and the visitors were assembled in the outer court. The hall was decorated in most
sumptuous style, with expensive rugs, and hangings of
fine linen, and tapestries of many colors wrought with
threads of gold. And for the support of the vast tent
which formed the hall there were pillars thirty feet high,
plated with silver and gold, and set with precious stones.
And around about the sides were costly portières, em-
broidered with figures and shot through with gold
threads, hung on gilded and silvered rods.

"The circuit of the court was half a mile. Everything
was started at the signal of a trumpet-blast, whether it
was the beginning of the feast, the celebration of the
marriages, or the pouring of one of the various libations,
so that all the army might know." "After the banquet,"
resumes Arrian,[1] "the brides entered and seated themselves each beside her fiancé, who thereupon took her
by the hand and kissed her; and the first to do this was
the king. . . . Then each man, taking his wife, led her
away. Their dowries Alexander gave to every one of
them. And he caused the names to be written down of
all the other Macedonians who had married Asiatic
women, and there were said to be over ten thousand of

[1] VII, 4, 7 f.

them. To these, too, gifts were given by Alexander at
the marriage feast."

For five consecutive days artists from every land and
people entertained the cosmopolitan assembly with dis-
plays of skill as various as were the ideas and interests
to which they catered. But the discord was lessened
and the dominant *motiv* repeated again and again by
the appearance and reappearance of the greatest Greek
masters of the dramatic and musical arts.

It being established by these many incidents that it
was a salient trait of Alexander's character to disclose
his fundamental policies by acts elaborately staged and
performed before the largest possible audiences, we may
return to his extraordinary visit to the temple of Ammon
of Cyrene. He had first to proceed one hundred and
seventy-five miles along the Libyan coast and then
southwest for about seven days before reaching his goal.
A month of the most difficult marching, at a time when
every day was precious, was the high price which Alexander thought it economical to pay for the recognition
which he there received as the son of Zeus. What was,
then, the value of this well-advertised recognition?

That it had none for Egypt and the nations of Asia,
to whom the god of Siwah, like the prophet in his own
country, was without honor, implies that Alexander
esteemed highly its value in the Greek world, where the
voice heard at Siwah was in fact an admonition to the

pious and might be an embarrassment to all in official positions. An oracle, however, was always addressed primarily to him who received it. Other persons could neglect it with impunity. Nevertheless, Alexander had made it improbable that anybody should be unaware that Zeus had acknowledged him as his son. Doubtless, much discussion was provoked; but there the matter seems to have ended so far as Hellas was concerned till seven years later, at the time of the feast at Susa, when Alexander issued a mandate to all the Greek city-states, new and old, that they should recognize him as a god.

Strange as it may seem to us, among whom church and state are separated sharply, and religion depends upon a revelation which can be interpreted but not sup-plemented, the question was one which came properly within the province of the general assembly of the citizens of each city. At this very time the Athenians, for example, had waiting within their gates many foreign deities whose claims to official recognition were being pressed upon the ecclesia by votaries among both the alien and the native population. Such were Isis the Egyptian, and the Cypriote Aphrodite. In compara-tively recent times, moreover, the ecclesia had yielded to similar solicitations, and had enrolled among the deities of the Athenian people Asclepius and the Thracian Bendis.

In a polytheistic world there is no logical limit to the

possible number of gods; so that the chance always existed that there were deities whom a given community had not yet discovered at any given moment. There is, in such a world, a logical necessity that anarchy should be absent from heaven. Hence each community had to rank its gods and goddesses according to their power and spheres of activity. The lowest god, demigod or hero was, accordingly, separated from mankind by no deep or broad chasm. With most of their deities, in fact, the Greeks were on terms of familiar intimacy, as were mediæval Christians with their saints. Various of the lesser gods, Theseus and Heracles among the ancestors of Alexander for example, had once been men who had been elevated to Olympus by the grace of Zeus because of the many services which they had rendered to men. It is true that they were the children of Zeus; but had not Zeus also claimed Alexander as his own son? Why, then, should not he too be deified?

The difficulty from the standpoint of religion — of the sentiment which had led in the past to the heroizing of men — was that he was still living. And this was an insurmountable difficulty. From the religious conceptions of the Greeks the worship of the living ruler could never be derived; and, in fact, it was by pious people and for theological reasons that the rendering of divine honors to Alexander was opposed in Athens and elsewhere.[1] The most that could be expected from men of

[1] In Macedon, by the regent Ἀντίπατρος, ἀσεβὲς τοῦτο κρίνας (Suidas).

religious convictions was a sullen acquiescence in something which they could not prevent.

The apotheosis of Alexander was grounded in impiety, in disbelief in the supernatural altogether. For the age in which he lived was marked by this very thing. In that time of storm and stress the ancient Greek religion became bankrupt. For enlightened people — and their name was then legion — the gods had ceased to have objective reality. Like the spirits of the departed whom Ulysses had recalled to consciousness by giving them blood to drink, they were dependent for their existence upon the kindliness of men. Without the ministrations of the living they would not merely be forgotten; they would be annihilated. It was the gratitude of mankind which had kept the memory of benefactors green by rites deemed and called religious. Once, to be sure, the deities had been real beings, but that was before they had died, while they were living upon the earth as men. Then they had performed great services — had founded cities, conquered worlds, established laws, invented arts, developed grains and fruits, and trained animals. So at least many men of talent and learning already taught. But it remained for Euhemerus of Messene, about fifty years later (*ca.* 280 B.C.), to give the idea classic expression in an entertaining work of popularization.[1] With all the circumstantiality of

---

[1] Pauly-Wissowa, *Real-encyclopädie*, VI, 1, pp. 952 *ff.*; Wendland, *Die Hellenistisch-römische Kultur* (1907), pp. 67 *ff.*

Defoe, he tells how, in the course of his voyaging, he was driven southward into the Indian Ocean from Araby the Blest, till he came to the island of Panchæa. There he found a model community whose social and political organization he described in the manner familiar to us from Plato's *Republic*. There, too, he made a remarkable discovery — an account written on golden tablets in "reformed Egyptian" by Hermes of the lives and achievements of Chronus, Zeus, and all the other gods and goddesses of the Greek hierarchy. They had been kings and notables of Panchæa, and some of them, like Zeus and Dionysus, had been world conquerors. Others, indeed, had earned the favorable verdict of posterity by very questionable acts. Aphrodite was the first prostitute, and Cadmus, the grandfather of Dionysus, was the cook of a king in Sidon and had run away with a flute girl named Harmonia.

This "sacred writ" was naturally the latest and most authoritative revelation. It was saved, moreover, from being a gospel of atheism because, as Cumont[1] says, "It left to the eternal and incorruptible stars . . . the dignity of original gods and exalted them in proportion as it lowered their rivals of bygone days." The signal merit of Chronus had been to introduce the worship of the heavenly bodies in Panchæa.

In this respect the *Scriptures* of Euhemerus accorded with a strong current of both earlier and contemporary

---

[1] *Astrology and Religion among the Greeks and Romans* (1912), p. 55.

religious thought. Most men at that time recognized supernatural powers of a certain sort, like Tyche, "Chance," — the favorite deity of the Hellenistic world, — whose play in human affairs modern disbelievers in religion also would be the last to deny. But they declined to recognize as efficacious the gods and goddesses in whose honor the cities maintained temples, priests, sacrifices, and games, except when they had lived on the earth as men and women.

At the best, therefore, these deities were simply prototypes of Alexander, who had founded seventy cities and given them their constitutions and laws, who had conquered all the territory which Dionysus had once overrun, and who was planning to build a highway along the coast of North Africa to the pillars set by Heracles at the limits of the world; who, moreover, was moulding the masses of Europe and Asia into a new race, and upheld, as no god had ever done, the social and political framework of the world.

Religion was unable to elevate a living man to godhood. Even in Egypt the sacred animals were but sacred animals till seventy days after their death, when they became deities. But irreligion, having degraded all gods to the level of human beings, had no reason to withhold from great men the homage which it accorded to the great dead.

The fundamental document on the deification of Greek kings comes to us stamped with the seal of the

Athenian state. It was sung by the multitude at the official reception of its sovereign, the young Macedonian king, Demetrius Poliorcetes, on his return to Athens in 290 B.C.[1] "The king comes, light-hearted as befits a god, fair and laughing, yet majestic withal in his circle of courtiers, he the sun, they the stars: hail! child of mighty Poseidon and of Aphrodite. The other gods are a long way off, or have no ears, or no existence, or take no care of us, but thee we see face to face—a true god, not one of wood and stone." This catchy bit of blasphemy makes it impossible for any reasonable doubt to linger as to the regions of thought from which the worship of Greek rulers sprang.

But why should men who regarded the gods they already had as useless burden the state with the cult of another whose power was only too real? Why abandon King Log for a possible King Stork? It is on this point chiefly that scholars disagree to-day. There are those who make the apotheosis of Alexander a tribute paid by the Greeks to transcendant genius, a result of the reverence-compelling personality of the man. I confess, however, that enthusiastic admiration such as this presupposes does not seem to me to harmonize with the contemptuous expressions which marked the establishment of his cult in certain places in Greece.[2] In Sparta, Damis moved, in regard to Alexander's message

---

[1] Ferguson, *Hellenistic Athens*, p. 143.
[2] Meyer, Ed., *Kleine Schriften*, p. 330, n. 2.

that he be decreed a god, that the Spartans "let him be called a god if he wishes it "; while in Athens Demosthenes advised his fellow-citizens "to acknowledge the king as the son of Zeus, or, for all he cared, as the son of Poseidon, if such was his pleasure." In other places, however, the recognition seems to have been spontaneous enough, and to have been an expression of real gratitude for services rendered or expected. But Greeks on earlier occasions, and other peoples as well, were equally grateful and no less servile without deifying the object of those sentiments. Why then did admiration, gratitude, or servility take this form in this particular instance?

It is true that deification was *demanded* of the Greek cities by Alexander, and that it was in response to a mandate sent out by him from Susa in 324 B.C. that "sacred ambassadors," such as were sent to gods and not to kings or states, arrived at Babylon in the spring of 323 B.C. a few weeks before Alexander's death, bearing the decrees in which his request was granted. But for the following fifty years it was at the initiative of the Greek cities, and, at times, against the will and interest of the recipient, that such honors were conferred upon later rulers. Hence we may be certain that in the first instance deification was an accommodation both to Alexander and to the cities in his realm. Nor can we, I think, be in serious doubt as to the character of the service it rendered.

It gave a legal position to Alexander in the world of city-states which he was organizing. It was unjust, Aristotle had taught him, that a man of supreme political capacity — such as he had displayed — should be treated as worthy of mere equality in the cities of his realm. Yet he could be treated in no other fashion if he were to be a citizen of them. On the other hand, now that he had freed himself from the constitutional limitations placed upon the earlier kings of Macedon and from the treaties which he had formed with the Hellenic cities at the opening of his reign, he ran the risk of being put to death or outlawed or ostracized, if he were not, as Aristotle suggested, rated as a deity upon the earth.

From his point of view, his rule was legitimatized when he was enrolled among the deities recognized by each city; for thereafter he had a clear right to issue orders to all the citizens of his world. From their point of view, on the other hand, by deifying Alexander they escaped from the intolerable necessity of obeying the commands of a foreigner. They thereby gave their consent to be ruled by him. They subordinated their will to his.

The deification of rulers was, accordingly, simply the proskynesis of cities. Its consequences were an absolutism such as Europe — and for that matter Asia — had never known before and has never ceased to know since. And it is this melancholy consequence of apotheosis which has only too frequently obscured its signal service: that it made possible the lasting union of all the city-states of the world in a single great territorial state.

SELECT BIBLIOGRAPHY

1. HOGARTH, D. *The Deification of Alexander the Great.* In *English Historical Review*, II (1887), pp. 317 *ff*.
2. NIESE, B. *Zur Würdigung Alexander's des Grossen.* In *Historische Zeitschrift*, LXXIX (1897), pp. 1 *ff*.
3. WHEELER, B. I. *Alexander the Great,* (1900).
4. BEVAN, E. *The Deification of Kings in the Greek Cities.* In *English Historical Review*, XVI (1901), pp. 625 *ff*.
5. MEYER, EDUARD. *Alexander der Grosse und die absolute Monarchie.* In *Kleine Schriften* (1910), pp. 283 *ff*.
6. KÄRST, J. *Der hellenistische Herrscherkult.* Beilage 2 in *Geschichte des hellenistischen Zeitalters*, II, 1 (1909), pp. 374*ff*.
7. FERGUSON, W. S. *Legalized Absolutism en route from Greece to Rome.* In *American Historical Review*, XVIII (1912), pp. 29 *ff*.

V

THE EMPIRE OF THE PTOLEMIES

THE death of Alexander the Great was followed by some days of indescribable confusion. When a certain semblance of order was restored the view was officially promulgated that he had not died at all, but had simply "departed from the life among men." His memory was, accordingly, not damned; and, in a sense, his presence in the world which he had transformed continued to be recognized. But not in any real sense. The imperial coins, wherever issued, bore for some time the great king's face as Zeus Ammon; but no imperial cult existed to bring steadily to men's consciousness the idea that their dead lord had an honored place among the Olympians. It was not by the will of those who succeeded to his power, but by the force of historic developments, that his *acta* were validated.

His heirs were the Macedonians whom he had recently tried to oust from their ancestral partnership with him. They were now to be found, partly in Macedon, partly in detachments throughout the empire, and partly in Babylon where Alexander had died. Those in Babylon took it upon themselves to act for the whole people; and what they did was to establish a regency in the interest of Philip Arrhidæus and the son whom Roxane was expected to bear, and to concur in the "grab" of the important western satrapies which was at once made by their chief officers.

It was they, too, who decided not to proceed with Alexander's ambitious projects. These, as read to them from his papers,[1] were "to build in Phœnicia, Syria, Cilicia, and Cyprus one thousand battleships of the super-trireme pattern for the campaign against the Carthaginians and the other peoples dwelling on the shores of the Mediterranean from Libya and Iberia clear round to Sicily; to construct a road along the coast from Cyrene to the Pillars of Hercules, and prepare harbors and naval stations at suitable places; to erect six temples at the enormous cost of $1,890,000 each (fifteen hundred talents); to found cities and transplant men and women both from Asia into Europe and from Europe into Asia, thus linking the two greatest continents by understandings based upon friendly intercourse and by brotherly feeling due to intermarriages." Alexander, it appeared, had looked upon his work as only half done: the Macedonians were eager to enjoy the fruits of an enterprise which they regarded as already finished.

Their sentiment was shared by Ptolemy, son of Lagos, formerly one of Alexander's aides. He had married a Persian princess at Alexander's order, but now he deserted her, and, taking his Athenian mistress, Thais,

---

[1] Diodorus, XVIII, 4.

with him, he went off to Egypt, which had been given to him as his province. There he established himself securely, governed with power and sagacity for forty years, and, marrying in succession two Macedonian princesses, founded a dynasty which gave to Egypt its last great queen, Cleopatra VI, and prior to her accession, ten kings,[1] all of whom were named Ptolemy. Between them they reigned two hundred and seventy-one years; the average length of the reign was over thirty-two years; several of them were expelled temporarily and several of them had colleagues, but nine of them died in possession of the throne. That constitutes a statistical record which it is hard to parallel in all history.

It would be a fascinating study of human enterprise and human depravity to trace the careers of these eleven monarchs. But to do so would be to exhaust the space at my disposal without reaching the special subject of my essay. It must suffice, therefore, to observe that the history of the Ptolemies falls into an imperial period of four reigns and one hundred and twenty years (323–203 B.C.); and a domestic period, likewise of one hundred and twenty years (200–80 B.C.), in which the native peoples, encouraged by the weakness of the Ptolemies abroad, and by a ruinous schism between the military and the civil elements of the foreign-resident population, gained point after point at the expense of the dynasty. A third period follows of fifty years' duration, in which

[1] Omitting the shadowy Eupator, Philopator Neos, and Alexander II.

Egypt was at the mercy, not now of the Roman Senate, but of the all-powerful generals who had dethroned it.

The last king of Egypt, Ptolemy the Piper, a bastard by birth and instinct, demeaned himself for twenty-eight years (80–52 B.C.); but by bankrupting his treasury and sacrificing the good opinion of his countrymen, he managed to transmit a badly tarnished crown to his famous daughter, then a girl of seventeen years.

Cleopatra VI had an asset of much greater value than the servility and buffoonery of her father, namely, her personal attractiveness. She early lost all repugnance against using her physical charms, as well as her even more notable mental graces, in what, with all our dislike for the imperial courtesan, we must characterize as her gallant and patriotic effort to rescue her country from the spoiler, to make the queen of Egypt the consort instead of the slave of the coming Roman monarch, to set proud Alexandria beside imperious Rome at the head of the Mediterranean peoples.

She gave herself to Julius Cæsar; bore him a son; left her kingdom and joined him in Rome, where Cicero and others paid her court in Cæsar's gardens, wondering, perhaps, if she was to become their titular queen. In contemporary documents Cæsar is called "the savior and benefactor of the inhabitable world"; and during the last year of his life he was busied with projects of universal empire. He meant to add the districts not yet Roman to his realm, to subdue the Getæ, the Scythians, and the Parthians. Why was not Egypt, the richest prize of all, included in the list of his intended conquests? It was the country which he had tried over twenty years earlier to secure as his own province. But that was before he had met Cleopatra. That he left it out of the military programme on which he was engaged at the time of his murder shows, I think, that Cleopatra's solution of the Egyptian question was likely to be his also.

Ten years later Alexandria witnessed an extraordinary spectacle.[1] On a stage plated with silver two thrones of gold stood, and on them sat side by side Antony as Dionysus and Cleopatra as Isis. At their feet sat Cæsarion, Cleopatra's son by Cæsar, and on a level with him Alexander, her oldest son by Antony, in Persian costume and with the tiara of the Persian kings. Lower down sat Alexander's twin sister, Cleopatra Selene, and at her side her younger brother, Philadelphus, in Macedonian costume and with the headgear of the kings of Macedon. The significance of the tableau Antony himself explained: Cleopatra, queen of Egypt, Cyprus, and Cœle-Syria, was henceforth 'queen of queens'; her son, Cæsarion, 'king of kings.' Alexander was declared king of Armenia and of the states lying between the Euphrates and India, Philadelphus, of Syria and all the lands between the Euphrates and the Hellespont, Cleopatra Selene, queen of Libya includ-

[1] Bouché-Leclercq, *Histoire des Lagides*, II, p. 278; Plut., *Antony*, 54; Dio Cassius, XLIX, 41.

ing Cyrene. It was the restoration of the ancient empire of the Ptolemies, and in Antony "captured Italy" was symbolized. The Alexandrian siren had regained what her ancestors had lost; and, had the Roman whom she had enthralled only proved equal to the task of maintaining his initial ascendency in Italy, she might, indeed, have fulfilled her boast and administered justice on the Capitol. But Antony went down to defeat at Actium and the young Augustus came to Egypt, like the comrades of Ulysses to the shore of the tempters, with his ears stuffed with wax.

Pascal[1] says: *Le nez de Cléopâtre : s'il eût été plus court, toute la face de la terre aurait changé.* But Pascal speaks as a philosopher. He probably did not know that Cleopatra had a prominent nose. He was certainly ignorant that her death made little or no difference in the constitutional position of Egypt. In a sense Augustus was simply the executor of the great queen's policy; for, after his reorganization of the Roman empire was completed, "it is," as Mommsen[2] says, "quite as correct to say that the kings of Egypt ruled in Rome as that the prince of the Roman people reigned in the valley of the Nile." Be that as it may, the empire of the Ptolemies could not have been recalled from the past even by the magic of a woman's

---

[1] *Pensées*, VI, 43 bis. Ed. Havet; cf. Bouché-Leclercq, *Hist. des Lagides,* II, p. 180, n. 1.

[2] *Gesammelte Schriften*, IV, p. 256.

beauty; for, as we shall see when we come to look at the second period of its history, the death it had died was a natural one. It had but experienced the fate to which its constitution made it prone. It was beset from its birth with incurable weaknesses.

None the less it made a brave show during the first century of its existence; and during the reign of its second monarch, Ptolemy Philadelphus (285–246 B.C.), its capital, Alexandria, was the London of the ancient world. Its only rival in trade and commerce was its neighbor to the west, Carthage. The golden age of the Ptolemies coincides with the one epoch in the history of the world in which Africa was the leader in business enterprise, in money power, in naval strength, in luxury, in science, and, till the real test came, in political prestige and influence. The commercial aristocracy of Carthage and the enlightened despots of Alexandria had the Mediterranean divided between them. West of Sicily lay a Carthaginian lake, into which foreign ships entered at their own peril; east of it, the chief harbors in the whole circuit from Cyrene to Corcyra, as well as the islands which lay in the area thus inclosed, the Ptolemies aimed to secure. Possession of the sea between Egypt and the Græco-Macedonian world and of the coasts which it washed and the islands which it surrounded, was the main object of the foreign policy of the early Ptolemies.

The founder of the dynasty was a brave soldier, but

a cautious general. Again and again he withdrew from
Asia before a land attack and put his main reliance
upon the natural defenses of Egypt. He was no sailor at
all; yet he became an admiral, and as the result of three
great maritime expeditions (308–306, 295–294, 288–
287 B.C.), he handed over to his unwarlike son the essential body of the possessions of the family outside of
Egypt. The founder of the dynasty was at the same
time the founder of the empire.

The Solomon of the Ptolemies, Philadelphus, is
addressed by Theocritus,[1] a Sicilian poet who had
recently come to Alexandria looking for a patron, in the
following adulatory strains: —

> "Lo he hath seen three hundred towns arise,
> Three thousand, yea three myriad; and o'er all
> He rules, the prince of heroes, Ptolemy.
> Claims half Phœnicia, and half Araby,
> Syria and Libya, and the Æthiops murk;
> Sways the Pamphylian and Cilician braves,
> The Lycian and the Carian trained to war,
> And all the isles; for never fleet like his
> Rode upon ocean: land and sea alike
> And sounding rivers hail King Ptolemy."

The hero of these lines had just brought a war against his
brother in Cyrene and his rival in Asia to a successful
termination (273 B.C.); and, except for a probable interval of four years (253–249 B.C.), the invincible fleet
which he then possessed ruled the sea till his death. But
he was anything but a warrior king. During his whole

---

[1] *Idyll*, XVII. (Translation of Calverley.)

life he never commanded an army or a fleet in person. Like Augustus Cæsar, with whom he has been compared, he had a delicate constitution which unfitted him for the rough and tumble of war. He had a lively intelligence, which was carefully cultivated, and, like the Emperor Hadrian, an insatiable thirst for novelties. A new book, an old painting, a strange animal, a useful invention, alike aroused his curiosity. One amazing woman — his own sister — swept him from his self-indulgent moorings. She made herself his wife — as any Egyptian woman might do with her brother — and, though she was his queen for six years at most (275–270 B.C.), when she was over forty and he over thirty-two, he followed her policy and cherished her memory for many long years.

That her *acta* might not be invalid he had her deified after her death, and that he might still be her consort, he had himself elevated at the same time to her side as the first self-constituted god-king since Alexander.

A sensualist by instinct, he surrounded himself in Alexandria with everything that appealed to his variegated lusts.[1] The women whom he took into his harem after his sister's death were given palaces and race-horses, public statues, — in costumes which were not always modest, — and even divine honors. Splendid new quarters were laid out in Alexandria, and public works erected there and elsewhere in his realm. The

---

[1] See Droysen, *Geschichte des Hellenismus*,[2] III, pp. 262 *ff*.

capital thronged with scientific, literary, and musical celebrities, attracted by the endowments and collections of the Museum, the richness of the library, the profusion of festivals, and the liberality of the king, who wished Alexandria to become to the new world what Athens had been to the old.

Yet despite all these manifold gratifications, life palled on the much-experienced monarch. He turned from the doctors to the quacks, and, shrinking from pain and death, experimented with draughts that were alleged to confer immortality: a strange act for one who was already a god! While suffering agony from the gout, he envied the lot of the fellahs, whom he saw from his window stretched out on the sand in the sun eating their simple meal. "Ye poor," he is said to have once exclaimed, "would that I had been one of you."

"From behind the rich curtains of his palace," as his stout adversary, Antigonus of Macedon,[1] phrased it, Ptolemy Philadelphus played cautiously and adroitly the great game of international politics. His emissaries, laden with gifts and money, were to be found at every capital from the Ganges to the Tiber. "Mighty kings" and "great cities," Theocritus tells us,[2] were in his pay; and in the harbor of Alexandria many great battleships lay ready to give emphasis to diplomacy, to support the agents whom his gold had brought into action.

By these means, too, he kept open the roads which

---

[1] Plut., *Aratus*, xv.   [2] *Idyll*, XVII, 110 f.

led across the sea from all directions to Alexandria; shut off, by a fringe of Egyptian possessions, the great continental empire of the Seleucids from access to the Mediterranean; and kept Greece so persistently in insurrection against its suzerain, Macedon, that he was able to ward off all danger from that quarter.

He enlarged his inherited empire by seizing Ionia when Eumenes I of Pergamum threw off the suzerainty of the Seleucids and shattered their authority in Asia Minor (263–261 B.C.); but the gains he then made he had to abandon during the upheaval which accompanied the revolt of his "son" in Ephesus (259–255 B.C.), and he suffered still further losses in Asia during the war he waged thereafter (253–249 B.C.), with Macedon and Syria combined. These, however, his son, Euergetes, at the opening of his reign (246–242 B.C.), regained, and he acquired districts in Ionia and the Hellespont besides; and the position which he thereby secured he held till his death twenty years later. On the sea, however, he showed himself less persistent than his father. Philadelphus had lost control of the Ægean when beaten at Cos in 253 B.C. by Antigonus of Macedon, but had not rested till he had regained it four years later, when the league of the Islanders, which was the immediate bone of contention, came again under the authority of his admirals. Euergetes suffered a crushing naval defeat in 242 B.C. off the island of Andros at the hands of the "veteran" Antigonus; whereupon he let the

Cyclades go altogether. That was not the only sequel,
however; for in consequence of the large outlay for little
gain entailed in building and keeping in readiness the
huge battleships then employed, and perhaps also in
consequence of the failure of the Carthaginians, despite
great naval expense and preparations, to hold the sea
against the improvised fleets of Rome in the First Punic
War (which had just ended), the third Ptolemy, like the
Barcid government in Carthage, abandoned the policy
of maintaining a fleet strong enough to drive all enemies
from their respective parts of the Mediterranean. It was
a great mistake in each case. When at the end of the
third century B.C. Macedon and Syria, the traditional
and long-suffering enemies of Egypt, were in a position
to renew their joint struggle with the Ptolemies, the far-
spread Ptolemaic empire fell together like a house of
cards, and Rome alone saved the dynasty from complete
destruction.

A variety of motives actuated the early Ptolemies in
their struggle for foreign dominions. Pride of possession
was among them, of course. The court poet Callima-
chus [1] struck a responsive chord when, in his poem on
the death of Arsinoë, the sister-wife of Philadelphus, he
has the sad news flashed from beacon point to beacon
point till it reaches Lemnos at the outer edge of the
empire. National honor is a strong motive for action,

---

[1] Wilamowitz-Moellendorff, *Sitzb. d. Berl. Akad.* XXIX (1912), pp. 524 *ff.*

but it is commonly stirred by the fear of losing something possessed rather than by the hope of acquiring something new. Hence we must look deeper for the reasons which led cautious statesmen like the first two Ptolemies to place round Egypt its girdle of power.

The motive suggested by Polybius [1] is quite different. It was with regard to possible movements on the part of the monarchs of Syria, Asia Minor, Thrace, and Macedon that the Ptolemies held, as he says, "the most important towns, places, and harbors along the whole coast" of the eastern Mediterranean. And there can be no doubt that he is right in attributing this rather malicious aim to them. They were, doubtless, great intriguers. But to Polybius, looking on from without, from one of the districts which had been affected by the close proximity of Egyptian garrisons and naval stations, the connection of these posts with the foreign policy of the Ptolemies was apt to obtrude itself to the exclusion of everything else. Nowadays historians are prone to a similar onesidedness because of the close attention they give to economic factors. They are quite right when they stress the importance of Ptolemaic naval power and of the vantage-points held in Europe and Asia for the development of Alexandrian commerce. The lighthouse which Ptolemy erected at the mouth of the Nile at a cost of a million dollars (eight hundred talents) was not only one of the seven wonders of the

[1] v, 34, 6–8.

world: it was a messenger of good will to the trading
vessels which came from all the dependencies with or
without cargoes, to get for Greek consumption the
varied products of the Alexandrian factories, the
Egyptian grain-fields, and the Nile-borne traffic of
Arabia, India, Somaliland, and Ethiopia. What the
lighthouse symbolizes, the growth of Alexandria to half
a million in a hundred years proves: the magnitude of
the commerce which the transmarine possessions of
Egypt stimulated, when they did not originate it.

Where the economic historians are wrong, however,
is in doing what Polybius did. *He* made the imperial
policy of the early Ptolemies primarily foreign; *they*
make it primarily commercial. The truth is that it was
dictated also by the plain necessities of the domestic
situation. Let us see what that was.

The first Ptolemy had stepped into the place of the
Pharaohs on Alexander the Great's death. The only
right he cared to acknowledge for the obedience of the
Egyptians was the right of conquest. As for them, we
may be sure that just as they created the myth that
Alexander was not really Philip's child, but a son begot-
ten from Olympias by either Nectanebus, the last native
Pharaoh, or Ammon, the great god himself who had
taken the form of Nectanebus for the purpose; and just
as they in later times represented Cæsar and Antony as
Ammon reincarnate, that Cleopatra's bastard children

might be legitimate Pharaohs: so, too, they applied to Ptolemy the fiction by which for thousands of years they had been wont to bridge over the gaps in the genealogy of their kings.[1]

The bridge was necessary, however; for, in their thinking, the gods, who had once lived among men, on withdrawing to the divine abodes, had left one of their number to rule over the world — which, of course, was Egypt. From him all their kings were descended. The Pharaoh was, accordingly, the only god who resided upon the earth, and, as such, fittingly the mediator between men and the great gods and goddesses of the upper and nether world.[2] The Pharaoh was, therefore, both the god-king and the chief priest. The whole land and people of Egypt were his property. Without his presence and ministrations the earth would literally languish and grow barren, and the men, women, and children would perish. Egypt was, accordingly, bound to have a legitimate Pharaoh. Ptolemy could be made Ammon's offspring as easily as Alexander the Great; but how it was done we do not know.

On his arrival in Egypt, Ptolemy found there two other states in addition to that of the Egyptians. These were the old Greek city of Naucratis and the new city of Alexandria. A third arose when he himself founded

---

[1] Bouché-Leclercq, *Histoire des Lagides*, III, pp. 1 *ff.*
[2] Breasted, J. H., *Development of Religion and Thought in Ancient Egypt* (1912).

Ptolemais to be to Upper Egypt what Alexandria was to
Lower Egypt — the centre and rallying point of Hellenic interests. To these three city-states he added a
multitude of others in and about the Mediterranean
when he acquired for his house its foreign dominions.
The convenient thing for these to do was to bind themselves to him by the Gordian knot of religious worship;
and, as Ptolemy Soter, or the Savior, he was in fact
enrolled in the circle of deities recognized by the several
cities. In Alexandria we may be sure that its founder,
Alexander the Great, had been accorded divine honors
from the beginning, and that after his death the citizens
appointed each year a priest of Alexander, just as they
had been in the habit of doing while he was alive, and
just as they appointed one for Zeus or Apollo. However,
at some date between 311 and 289 B.C., perhaps on his
assumption of the regal title in 306 B.C., Ptolemy took
into his own hands the administration of his capital, and
thenceforth appointed personally the priest of the city-
god Alexander, who became therewith an imperial god.
To this cult Philadelphus did not add that of his parents, "the savior gods," when he had them officially
deified at their death (283 B.C.); but he did add to it that
of his deceased queen and of himself when in 270 B.C.
he inaugurated the worship of "the brother gods." His
example was followed by each succeeding pair of rulers
to the end of the dynasty, except that the savior gods
were inserted by the fourth Ptolemy in their proper

place after Alexander. So that central among the gods of the capital of the empire stood ultimately the long series of the departed rulers and at its head the living king and queen.

Outside the capital, in the city-states of the realm, as later on in the provinces subject to the Roman emperors, the reigning monarchs were alone the recipients of divine honors. The living Ptolemy, by recognizing the divinity of his predecessors, assumed responsibility for the validity of all their *acta*. They had issued their mandates (*prostagmata*) as gods; so long as they remained gods their mandates must be obeyed. The cities, on the other hand, had no concern except to legalize the orders issued to them by their living rulers, once their living rulers had legalized and thus become responsible for all orders issued by the dead. At Rome the memory of certain emperors was damned, and their acts rescinded. That was possible there because the emperor was theoretically only an officer of the Roman people. One means employed to invalidate the *acta* of deposed rulers was to refuse to have them among their gods after their death. The Alexandrians had no such discretion. After about 306 B.C. they were subjects themselves, not masters, of the Ptolemies. In their city it was the living Ptolemy who willed his own deification, and he could withhold divine honors from his predecessor only when, as in the solitary case of the founder of the dynasty, the monarch neglected to have himself created a god

during his lifetime. Since his wish was decisive, it is
not surprising that he had the members of his family,
his wife, sisters, children, and concubines, elevated to
Olympus along with himself. Curiously enough, however, Philadelphus and his four immediate successors,
while demanding that their subjects should worship
them as deities, treated themselves simply as kings, and
carefully refrained from describing themselves as gods
even in their public communications. The fact seems
to be that only by accepting the Egyptian theory of a
divine incarnation could the Ptolemies find a theological
ground for constituting themselves gods. This concession to native thinking the proud early members of the
dynasty refused, however, to make, preferring to
challenge by their own self-denial the divine honors
which they required from others. With this view accords
the further fact that the first Ptolemy deliberately to
court a native support for his throne — Euergetes II —
was also the first to sign his edicts as θεός, or "god."

While it is true that no great empire ever existed
without a constitutional fiction, it is also true that it
never endured on a fiction alone. The Macedonian
soldiers whom Ptolemy found in Egypt and those whom
he brought with him and sent for later were essential for
the maintenance of his government. So long as the son of
Alexander the Great lived, and, indeed, for four years
longer (till 306 B.C.), Ptolemy was simply their general.
Then he became their king, and to legitimatize this

practical usurpation, the legend arose that he was not really the son of Lagos, but the son of Philip. It is to the honor of Ptolemy that he had nothing to do with this libel on the good name of his mother, and preferred rather to be an illegitimate king than an illegitimate son. Besides, it was only necessary to go back a generation or two to attach the line of Ptolemy to that of the ancient "Zeus-born" kings of Macedon. The wife of Lagos had belonged, in fact, to the royal family, as the Ptolemies took good care to observe.

The Ptolemaic empire was, accordingly, based on three concurrent theories, one for the native Egyptians, one for the Greek city-states, and one for the Macedonians.

Appian of Alexandria,[1] writing about two hundred years after the death of Cleopatra, cites the royal registers as authority for his report that Philadelphus kept, for land operations 200,000 foot, 40,000 cavalry, and arms for 300,000 men; in addition, 300 war elephants and 2000 war chariots; for naval warfare, 2000 transports, 1500 battleships with three to five banks of rowers, and oars and rigging for twice that number. He had also, according to the same authority, 800 royal barges with gilt poops and beaks, and in his treasury a reserve of 740,000 Egyptian talents, or $890,000,000.

That the reserve as given amounts to three times the

---

[1] *Prooem.* 10. Tarn, *Antigonus Gonatas*, pp. 454 *ff.*

value of the gold and silver in the United States treasury shows that the enumeration belongs only in the history yet to be written of the absurdities of statistics. More credible estimates of the Egyptian army place it at 80,800 under the second Ptolemy and (exclusive of natives, who then numbered 26,000) 49,700 under the fourth Ptolemy.[1] These are very large totals. It will help to solve many questions of Ptolemaic policy to observe where the soldiers came from.

But first we may notice that they could not come from the natives; for their most important duty was to hold them in subjection. There were so many people to keep down! Alexandria itself had a large native quarter. The other two Greek cities in the land were but alien flecks in the midst of a great multitude. Up and down the valley lay the native hamlets, to the number of 33,333 according to Theocritus, teeming with the seven million people whom Egypt then sustained. Alexander the Great may have dreamed of Hellenizing these masses; Ptolemy, however, had no such thought, as is shown conclusively by the fact that under his dynasty and, indeed, for at least two centuries after its fall, Naucratis, and probably also Ptolemais, forbade by law marriages between their citizens and the natives.[2]

The sole landowner in Egypt was the king. The entire valley of the Nile was literally his personal estate.

---

[1] Athenæus, v, 202 f.; Polybius, v, 65.
[2] Wilcken, *Grundzüge*, 13. 17, 47.

Except for certain portions "set apart" for particular purposes, which we shall examine in a moment, the arable land surrounding the countless native villages was in the possession of tenants of the crown, who paid to the king about seven bushels of grain per acre as rent and sowed their land according to royal orders with seed provided by him; who might be dispossessed at any time, but could neither abandon their plots (at least in seeding- and harvest-time) nor their villages (except for short periods), at their own volition; who had numerous services in connection with "geometry," irrigation, transport, post, and similar matters to perform, and might be moved or forced en masse to redeem and cultivate dry or marsh land situated near their hovels; who paid a poll-tax and a house-tax to the king, and one sixth of the yield of their vineyards and orchards, when they had any, to the temple authorities whom the king appointed; who bought their beer, oil, fish, honey, cloth, soda, bricks, wood, paper, and almost every other article of common use either exclusively from the king, who was the sole producer and seller, or in certain cases from private dealers, who, however, paid so much for their license that they could not undersell the king. Watchmen were everywhere in the fields to see that the king was not defrauded. Gendarmes patrolled the country to guard the roads and deserts, to prevent smuggling and "moonshining." Scribes and bankers were in every village to keep account of all changes in families and in leases; to visé every payment. Every village had its storehouse of records, of grain, of money. And on the Nile went to and fro the royal transports which carried the surpluses to Alexandria, and the products of the royal factories to the local depots from which they were sold. The king of Egypt was, accordingly, by far the greatest merchant and manufacturer in the whole world. Even in far distant Delos the price of paper, myrrh, and other articles was fixed by the pleasure of the royal monopolist. That his interference "regulated the market" to his own advantage may be inferred from the fact that the sheet of paper which was sold in 296 B.C. for one obol (three and one half cents) cost on the average eleven in 279–250 B.C.[1]

Thus set about by countless officials and shorn to the very skin, the fellahs lived under the Ptolemies, "patient, laborious, cheerful," yet filled with hidden bitterness at the magnificence in which their masters lived at their expense in Alexandria, venting their rage in impotent prophecies that "the great city at the water's edge should become a drying-place for the nets of fishers, and its gods should migrate to the native capital Memphis."[2]

Clearly, the army of the Ptolemies could not be recruited from such elements. The Egyptians might be put on the warships as rowers, used in the transport service, and, occasionally when the need was great, in

---

[1] Glotz, *Journal des Savants* (1913), pp. 16 *ff.*
[2] Wilcken, *Grundzüge*, 22.

small numbers as soldiers. But granted that they might
be useful in fighting abroad, — at home they belonged
to the enemy from whom the early Ptolemies had greatly
to fear.

As such, the citizens of Alexandria, Naucratis, and
Ptolemais were apparently exempt from military service.
Hence the great problem of national defense could not
have been solved by the founding of new Greek cities of
this type in Egypt had there been room for them, or by
the founding of any kind of cities, had Ptolemy thought
it possible to organize the natives in urban communities
round a Greek or Macedonian nucleus — as Alexander
may have wished to do, as the Romans in fact did in the
year 202 A.D.; for, even if Ptolemy had cared for that
kind of thing, the Greek or Macedonian nucleus did not
as yet exist in Egypt. It had to be brought there from
abroad. Hence it was a question of life and death for
the Ptolemaic dynasty to remain in constant communi-
cation with the regions of the eastern Mediterranean
whence came supporters of their rule, soldiers for their
armies.

"But shouldst thou really mean a voyage out," says
one Greek peasant to another in Theocritus,[1] —

> "The freeman's best paymaster 's Ptolemy.
>   (Æschines)
>   What is he else?
>   (Thyonichus)
>   A gentleman: a man

[1] *Idyll*, 14, 58 *ff*. (Translated by Calverley.)

Of wit and taste: the top of company;
Loyal to ladies; one whose eye is keen
For friends, and keener still for enemies.
Large in his bounties, he, in kingly sort,
Denies a boon to none: but, Æschines,
One should not ask too often. This premised,
If thou wilt clasp the military cloak
O'er thy right shoulder, and with legs astride
Await the onward rush of shielded men:
Hie thee to Egypt."

Phœnicia and its hinterland were necessary to Ptolemy because of their forests of timber for shipbuilding, which Egypt lacked. The rest of his transmarine possessions were necessary because of their stock of reliable soldiers, which Egypt also lacked. Hence, as stated already, the imperial policy of the early Ptolemies was a plain consequence of their domestic policy — of holding Egypt as a foreign country.

Let us now see what they did with the store of soldiers which they possessed and with the new recruits whom they constantly added to it.[1] I have already drawn your attention to certain lands which the Ptolemies "set aside" for particular purposes. One complex of such lands they assigned to the temples. And I may remark that while the Ptolemies appointed and controlled the priests, they also conciliated them, by leaving them valuable perquisites, paying to them stated sums annually, building new temples and repairing old ones, and allow-

---

[1] For the following section the works of Rostowzew, Bouché-Leclercq (vol. IV), Wilcken, and Lesquier cited in the Select Bibliography at the end of this chapter are fundamental.

ing them to make for their own consumption the various articles which they could buy only at the royal counters and at monopolistic prices. They also set their land aside in a favored category. What is common to this category is not a single fiscal arrangement, but a relinquishing by the king of his right of direct management. To its members he binds himself in a way that does not impair his ownership, but does restrict his ability to take possession.

To this category belong the "gifts" of large blocks of land with their villages to his courtiers, who received them free from rent and taxes. The "friends" of the Ptolemies, though they resided in Alexandria, were thus landed proprietors, absentee landlords, who maintained their luxurious establishments in the capital on the rents which their Egyptian tenants paid. Common soldiers could not expect to become feudal lords by entering Ptolemy's service. But for his "loyal comrades," as Theocritus[1] calls them, — his officers, court dignitaries, and favorites, — he had such benefices to confer.

To the ordinary men-at-arms lots of land all over Egypt were assigned; to those of the guard and the cavalry, sixty-five and forty-five acre farms, to the infantrymen, farms of twenty acres. For Egyptian conditions these were very large units, and since under Philadelphus — who perfected this system of farming out his soldiers — the army consisted of 57,600 foot and

[1] *Idyll*, XVII, III.

23,200 horsemen, over one quarter of all the arable land in Egypt would have been in their possession, if only land naturally watered by the Nile had been given to them, and if none of them were mercenaries serving only for hire. Many, however, were doubtless mercenaries of this type; and to the rest, land was commonly distributed which needed some expenditure of capital and energy to be reclaimed from the desert or the water. Of this kind of land the Ptolemies evidently inherited a goodly quantity from the Persians, whose government had been rendered inefficient in the fourth century B.C. by frequent revolts of the natives.

The soldiers might sublet their lots in whole or part and live in Alexandria or elsewhere. Or they might take possession and till them with their own hands. To facilitate the actual distribution of the army over the country, the king attached to the lots "quarters" on the premises of the neighboring Egyptians. This was not at all to the liking of the latter, as the following letter of a quartermaster to a county official shows:[1] "We have discovered that certain owners of houses in Crocodilopolis, which were once used for quartering troops, have taken off the roofs, and walled up the doors and built altars in their places. This they have done so as not to have them occupied. If then you agree, in view of the shortage of quarters, write Agenor that he make the owners of the houses take the altars down, and build them up

[1] Wilcken, *Chrestomathie*, 449.

again better than before upon the most suitable and conspicuous parts of the roofs, so that we may be able to take possession." The gods had never objected to having old altars replaced by finer ones. Henceforth, not the entrances, but the roofs, were to be protected by religion. The ancient quartermaster knew his business.

It was decidedly to the interest of the government that it should have a sort of garrison in residence in all the *nomes*, or counties, of Egypt — trained soldiers ready to take their places in their companies at the command of the chief nome official, who was also their general.

These men were by no means all Macedonians or Greeks. Some of them were Persians who had been in the land when Ptolemy arrived; some were Libyans, Jews, Thracians, Mysians, Galatians; nearly all were from the regions tapped by the empire of the Ptolemies.

They paid no rents for their lots, no poll-tax, and one tenth, in place of one sixth, of the yield of their gardens and orchards. Like the Hellenes generally, they might give commutation money in lieu of manual labor on dykes and canals. In other respects they were taxed rather more severely than the "royal tenants"; and, in addition, they had to pay certain feudal "aids" to the king. If they failed to pay these "aids," or if they fell in arrears with their taxes, they lost their holdings. Hence they were under a financial constraint to make the land, which they commonly received as waste land, productive. The soldiers were, accordingly, the "pioneers" of Ptolemaic Egypt, steadily at work enlarging the arable areas of the country and redressing the agricultural wrongs which it had sustained during the troubles of the later Persian régime.

Their lots reverted to the king when they died or left the army. The king could then add them to his domain or reassign them to other soldiers. During the imperial period of Ptolemaic history he seems to have taken the former course whenever the land was in a condition to bring him in a rent in addition to the taxes. However, from the very beginning, he undertook to make a new or a re-grant to the sons of dead or superannuated soldiers who were trained for military service. These were officially designated "men of the *epigone*, or increase," and they entered the army at the same time that they entered upon their inheritance. In this way the Ptolemies bred a crop of new soldiers in Egypt, so that they might look forward to being gradually less dependent upon mercenaries recruited from beyond the seas. Egypt was being enriched by a new military caste which should take the place by the side of the new dynasty which the "*machimoi*" or "warriors" had occupied during the old days of the native Pharaohs.

Multiracial though the soldiers were, they all spoke Greek. They had to regulate their private conduct and their business affairs by the special laws established in Egypt for the benefit of the various ethne, or nationalities, to which they belonged. For in Ptolemaic Egypt, as in the Turkish empire to-day, foreigners brought their own legal restrictions and safeguards with them, which, however, were formulated, for use in the Ptolemaic courts, in ethnic codes. These codes, however, were either couched originally in Greek, or, like the laws of Moses, which the Jews observed, they were translated into Greek at an early date. How much political freedom the various nations enjoyed, it is difficult to say; but in general they seem to have tempered the absolutism of the Ptolemies only where they were massed together in large numbers, as in Memphis and, above all, Alexandria. Elsewhere the ethnic groups were, doubtless, constituted chiefly of the territorial soldiers, or *cleruchs*, as they were called.[1] These, however, ceased to have any civil rights when called by the king into active service. With them political agitation could become effective only when it became mutiny.

Prominent among the institutions which the Hellenic and Hellenized foreigners brought into Egypt were those that centred in the gymnasia. Some of them were, doubtless, at first and for long, a subject of scandal and wonderment to the natives. As the Greeks ran and tumbled stark naked in the palæstræ, or in the contests

---

[1] See for this section Lesquier, *op. cit.*, pp. 142 *ff.*; Mitteis, *Grundzüge Einl.* XII; Schubart, W., *Spuren politischen Autonomie in Ægypten unter den Ptolemäern, Klio*, x (1910), pp. 41 *ff.*; cf. *Id. Archiv für Papyrusforschung*, v, pp. 81 *ff.*; Jouguet, P., *La vie municipale dans l' Égypte Romaine* (1911); Plaumann, G., *Ptolemais in Oberægypten* (1910).

for which, as for the army, the palæstræ were the train-
ing-grounds, the story of Heracles and Busiris was constantly reënacted; except that in time Busiris came to
see whence sprang the strength which he could not
resist. It was in the gymnasia also that the Greeks
received their higher education and by its means that
they secured for their sons the ideas which the poetry
and philosophy of Hellas alone could give. In the gymnasia temples of Hellenism appeared in county after
county of Egypt.

The foreigners brought with them into Egypt their
native religions, and, when they were not monotheists
like the Jews, they came easily into sympathy with the
myriad cults of the natives. A religious *rapprochement*
was thus established and a bi-religious *milieu* created,
by which a new half-Greek, half-Egyptian god, Sarapis,
whom Ptolemy I introduced from Sinope, prospered.
Before long this Janus-like deity, who was endowed with
a sanctity and miraculous power which hoary Egypt
could alone give, and with a plastic beauty peculiarly
Greek, became distinctively *the* great god of Egypt, and,
in conjunction with Isis, Anubis, and Harpocrates, the
most active religious force in the whole world of the
Ptolemaic empire. Sarapis-Osiris, the monarch, judge,
and savior of the world of the dead: Ptolemy-Pharaoh,
the monarch, judge, and savior of the world of the living; — these two and these two alone received the divine homage of Greeks and Egyptians alike. The early

Ptolemies willed the impossible; to accept the native deities, cults, creeds, and hierarchies as the active element in the fused Græco-Egyptian religion; to let the two civilizations represented in their realm coalesce in so far as their religious ideas, practices, aspirations, and hopes were concerned; and at the same time to keep them apart in other respects: to preserve in other matters the unapproachable superiority of the invaders.

Certainly, success in this attempt to graft the ancient religion which he as Pharaoh was bound to accept and preserve on the new stock of Hellenism without corrupting the fine flavor of the fruit hitherto borne by it in Greece, depended on making the Greek cities, Alexandria, Naucratis, and Ptolemais, and the Græco-Macedonian military colonies simply the Egyptian portion of a Græco-Macedonian realm reaching over the seas to the head of the Ægean. This necessary support to his position in Egypt the third Ptolemy jeopardized when he neglected to replace the great fleet after 242 B.C. For twenty long years, moreover, he left his army at work farming in Egypt, with the inevitable result that it became immobile. Such a neglect of military matters seemed warranted by the impotence of his two great rivals. For during this entire period Asia was rent by a dynastic struggle and Macedon was paralyzed by a general insurrection in Greece. His weak and indolent son paid the penalty for his father's neglect. By strengthening his army with 26,000 natives, whom he armed and drilled in the Macedonian fashion (221–217 B.C.), he saved the empire for seventeen years, when it fell before the combined attack of Macedon and Syria (202–200 B.C.); but he tempted the Egyptians to lay claim with the sword to partnership with the foreigners in the government. Thus presented, their claim was rejected, as was natural; but once the empire was lost and the flow of immigration into Egypt ceased, the Ptolemies of the "domestic" period were forced to acknowledge its justice.

They constituted their territorial army more and more from native soldiers, to whom they gave increasingly larger lots, while they progressively diminished the size of those held by the foreigners. They ceased to take back the holdings on the death or superannuation of the occupants, thus admitting the right of sons and other male descendants to get, in return for military service, not dry or marsh land, as in the early days, but land already redeemed by their father's capital and labor. Soldiers ceased to be soldiers spending their spare time winning new land from the desert and the swamp for their master's estate; and became farmers to whom service in the army was a nuisance and a loss. The army became thereby hopelessly immobile.

The age was generally one of economic decline and not of economic advance; for Egypt had gained more, as the sequel proved, from the vigorous government of

the early Ptolemies than it had lost by the expenditure
of its surpluses on the empire. In this decadent age
the Egyptians gained admission freely to the police and
administrative service as well as to the army. Thus
elevated in social esteem, they were able to intermarry
with their ancient lords; so that a considerable half-
breed and bilingual population developed — Greek in
the outward things, fellaheen, according to Polybius,
in character and culture. Alexandria, he says,[1] "three
strata occupy: the Egyptian and the native race, sharp
and (un)civilized. Then the mercenary troops, oppres-
sive and numerous and dissolute; for from old custom
they kept armed troops who had learned to rule rather
than to obey, on account of the worthlessness of the kings.
The third stratum was that of the Alexandrians, nor was
even this truly a civilized population owing to the same
causes, but yet better than the other two, for though
of mixed breed, yet they were originally Greeks, with
traditions of the general type of the Greeks. But this
part of the population having disappeared mainly owing
to Ptolemy Euergetes Physkon (145–116 B.C.) in whose
reign Polybius visited Alexandria, — for Physkon, when
revolted against, over and over again let loose his troops
on the population and massacred them, — and such
being the state of things, to visit Egypt was a long and
thankless journey." Foreign enemies the omnipotent
Roman Senate kept off during the second century B.C.

[1] XXXIV, 14 (Translated by Mahaffy, *The Ptolemaic Dynasty*, p. 191.)

But unnerved by the menacing patronage of the great
republic, the Ptolemies, now represented by men of
vigor and no character or of character and no vigor;
by women, who were sprung mostly from adelphic
unions, of remarkable ability, beauty, and morals, prefaced with a period of long-continued dynastic and national strife the dramatic epoch of Ptolemy the Piper
and Cleopatra the Great.

SELECT BIBLIOGRAPHY

1. MAHAFFY, J. P. *The Empire of the Ptolemies* (1895), and
   The Ptolemaic Dynasty (1899).
2. BELOCH, J. *Griechische Geschichte*, III (1904).
3. BOUCHÉ-LECLERCQ, A. *Histoire des Lagides*, especially
   vols. III and IV (1906).
4. ROSTOWZEW, M. *Studien zur Geschichte des römischen
   Kolonates* (1910).
5. WILAMOWITZ-MOELLENDORFF, ULRICH VON. *Staat und
   Gesellschaft der Griechen: D. Die makedonischen Königreiche* (1910).
6. LESQUIER, J. *Les institutions militaires de l'Égypte sous les
   Lagides* (1911).
7. KORNEMANN, E. *Ægypten und das (römische) Reich.* In
   Gercke and Norden's, *Einleitung in die Altertumswissenschaft* (1912), pp. 272 ff.
8. MITTEIS, L., und WILCKEN, U. *Grundzüge und Chrestomathie der Papyruskunde* (1912).

VI

THE SELEUCID EMPIRE

THE main portion of the conquests made by Alexander the Great lay in the continent of Asia. On the establishment of the regency this vast district had been divided among over twenty satraps. Ten years afterwards, in the fall of 313 B.C., one of these, Antigonus, known in history as Monophthalmus, or the "One-eyed," had now held for two years all the territory that lay between the fan-shaped offshoots of the Himalaya Mountains and the sea. The whole Asiatic coast of the Mediterranean from the Hellespont to Gaza on the Egyptian frontier was in his possession. His fleet ruled the sea.

The spring of 312 B.C. was one of the most critical moments in ancient history. In Antigonus the man seemed come with the will, ability, and power to take the place of Alexander. By his side stood a son of remarkable attractiveness and brilliancy, Demetrius, surnamed Poliorcetes, or "Taker-of-Cities"; so that a dynasty seemed assured.

The work to be done was plainly indicated and preparations for its accomplishment were already completed. After having stirred up an insurrection in Greece in the preceding year, the fleet of Antigonus had joined his main army which was massed at the Hellespont in readiness to cross into Europe for the conquest of Thrace and Macedon. In this district Antigonus conducted operations in person. His son Demetrius was stationed with a minor army in Palestine with instructions to avoid an engagement, and simply to keep Ptolemy cooped up in Egypt till the European campaign was ended. If beaten in his attack on Thrace and Macedon, Antigonus had nothing serious to fear so long as he was master of the sea; if victorious, he could then fall with irresistible force upon Egypt and complete the unification of Alexander's empire. The whole campaign was admirably planned and the troops well distributed for its successful execution.[1]

That it did not even get started was partly due to Ptolemy, who, impelled by the magnitude of his danger, took the desperate step of adding many natives to his army; and partly due to Demetrius, who, despite his numerical inferiority, his instructions, and the judgment of his staff officers, risked a pitched battle at Gaza, and was decisively defeated. That the project could never again be renewed on similarly advantageous terms was due to Seleucus, the son of Antiochus. For taking a thousand men with him this accomplished officer, old in service though still young in years, set out straightway after the battle of Gaza for Babylon, his own satrapy, whence he had fled to Egypt for fear of Antigonus four years earlier. Ten years afterwards, in 302 B.C., when

[1] Kromayer, *Historische Zeitschrift*, c, p. 50.

Antigonus again proceeded to conquer Macedon and Thrace, after having beaten Ptolemy back into Egypt, his great aim was frustrated, not only because the king of Thrace, Lysimachus, outmanœuvred him by getting an army across into Asia Minor, but also because Seleucus, now master of all the territory in the rear of Antigonus between the Euphrates and the frontiers of India, threw the decisive weight of his new army into the scale, and joined Lysimachus in crushing their common enemy at the great battle of Ipsus in 301 B.C.

Thereby Seleucus advanced his western frontier from the Euphrates to the edge of the Mediterranean, shifted his capital from Babylon to newly founded Antioch, and brought his empire into immediate proximity with the districts whence alone Greek and Macedonian immigrants could come. The Seleucids dated the founding of their dynasty from the return of Seleucus to Babylon in 312 B.C. There is, however, much to be said for the view that their empire was first established after the battle of Ipsus.

For the next twenty years (301–281 B.C.) Seleucus had the great good fortune to remain in secure possession of the vast territory which called him king; and while he failed to pass on to his descendants all the fruits of his crowning victory over Lysimachus at Corupedion in 282 B.C., he left to his son Antiochus I, surnamed Soter, or the Savior, and he in turn about twenty years later, to *his* son Antiochus II, surnamed Theos, or the

God, the fabric of their dominions, somewhat tattered at the edges, to be sure, but otherwise whole.

The evil genius of the Seleucid empire during the century when it was a great power was a woman — Laodice, the wife of Antiochus II and mother of his successor, Seleucus II, surnamed Callinicus, or the Glorious Victor (246–226 B.C.). Her power as queen is attested by other evidences, and also by the fact that she was associated with the king in the worship accorded by the satrapies of the realm to their rulers, every satrapy being required by Theos to establish a chief-priesthood in her especial honor.[1] None the less, she had to yield her place to Berenice, daughter of Ptolemy Philadelphus, when that crafty monarch seduced her husband from his alliance with Macedon by giving to him along with his daughter a prodigious dowry and extensive territorial concessions (249 B.C.). She retired to Asia Minor, where she owned large estates secured in earlier days at the expense of the royal domain, and where she could live in almost regal state. For the death of her former husband, which occurred three years later, she was probably not responsible, — though rumor held her guilty, — since Theos had already, on his deathbed apparently, and for reasons of sound dynastic policy, designated her oldest son, then

---

[1] Dittenberger, *Orientis Græcæ Inscriptiones Selectæ*, 224; if the king is Antiochus II, and not, as is now claimed (Pozzi, *Memorie della Reale Accademia di Torino*, serie II, tom. LXIII, p. 345, n. 4), Antiochus III. See, however, Kärst, *Geschichte des hellenistischen Zeitalters*, II, I, p. 422 and Bouché-Leclercq, *Hist. des Séleucides*, pp. 90 f., 470 ff.

a "youth nearing manhood," as his successor, to the exclusion of the boy with whom his Egyptian queen had recently presented him. Nor is she to be condemned harshly for having had her rival and her son's rival put out of the way; for she acted not only in self-defense, but also to save the Seleucid empire from becoming simply an appanage of Egypt during the long minority of Berenice's child. For conducting to a successful termination, despite initial disasters, the campaign against Ptolemy III, by which she put her son in possession of his throne, she is deserving of high credit. It was when this was accomplished, and her son was king, that her ambition led her into maternal and political crime; for, in order to retain the government, which her oldest son, now arrived at years of discretion, threatened to take from her, she set up against him her younger son Antiochus, surnamed the Hawk, for whom she got the administration of Asia Minor. The Seleucids became thereby divided against themselves, and for twenty years (242–223 B.C.) they were so weakened by a dynastic feud that they not only neglected vital questions of foreign policy, but had to permit the total loss of certain frontier satrapies and the rebellion of almost all the rest. Antiochus III, surnamed the Great, opened his reign with an error — the attempt to deal with the foreign situation before he had put his house in order; and he ended it with a great disaster — his irreparable defeat by the Romans at Magnesia in 190 B.C.; but in between he restored his authority over what Bevan in his *House of Seleucus* calls "the essential body of the Empire" and his suzerainty over its "outside sphere." The latter he accomplished by an impressive campaign, in Armenia (where ruled Xerxes, betrayed by his name as an Iranian), in Parthia (where Arsaces, the third king of a barbarian line from the Turanian desert, which had mastered that country a little less than forty years before, had just come to the throne), in Bactria (where Euthydemus, a Greek from Magnesia, had recently founded a new Hellenic dynasty in the place of an old one established nearly fifty years earlier by Diodotus, "lord of the thousand Bactrian cities," as he is called), and in India, where a certain Sophragasenus, following the examples of Arsaces and Euthydemus, recognized the superior power of the Seleucid.

On his return to Antioch after five years of marching and fighting in the Far East (210–205 B.C.), Antiochus wrested Palestine from the now feeble grasp of the Ptolemies. This exploit gave him the long-desired, long-lacked, and long-fought-for access to the sea; and for the first time in the history of the realm an opportunity was secured for the construction of a great fleet. Simultaneously, Philip of Macedon fell before the Romans at Cynocephalæ (197 B.C.); whereupon Antiochus went vigorously to work dislodging all "foreigners" from the Mediterranean seaboard of Asia Minor. This led in 192 B.C. to conflict with Rome.

Antiochus the Great has been late in coming into his due.[1] The mere fact that Hannibal, whom the undying hatred of Rome had driven into his service, worked out for him a plan of campaign against the Romans which he rejected, and that he put the greatest general of his age in charge of a new squadron of his extemporized fleet, have sufficed to rule out of court in advance any apology for his defeat. The issue showed that the view taken by Hannibal of the power of Rome was right. It is true that it could have been checked only by a great combination of all the Mediterranean states. But it is equally true that such a combination was impracticable. Antiochus had to deal with the situation as he found it. He risked too much for a few frontier districts and a possible hegemony in Greece. But he seems to have greatly underestimated the power of Rome, and to have credited the Senate with far less energy and tenacity of purpose than it actually possessed. Once his vanguard was thrown out of Greece by the incomparable Roman legions, his main hope of defending Asia Minor did actually rest with his fleet. Hannibal was, accordingly, in the right place. But the fleet was too new and too weak as well as too scattered to hold the Romans in Europe; and, once the veterans of the Second Punic War were across the Hellespont, no army in Asia could have resisted them.

The Seleucids learned a terrible lesson on the battle-

---

[1] See now Kromayer, *Hannibal und Antiochus der Grosse* (*Neue Jahrbücher für d. klass, Altert.* XIX (1907), pp. 681 *ff.*).

fields of Thermopylæ and Magnesia: the fatality was
that all the peoples in Asia learned it also. That Antiochus the Great consented to surrender all his possessions
in Asia Minor and to pay to the Romans an indemnity
of one thousand talents a year for twelve years; to hand
over his battleships and to limit his fleet to ten decked
vessels and a few small craft; to give up all his war elephants and to keep no others in the future; to take no
Italians into his service as mercenaries, and to throw
open his empire to the merchants and traders from
Rhodes, proclaimed only too clearly to the Orientals
that the days of the lordship of the Macedonians in the
world were past.

It was not, however, till after the untimely death of
his son, Antiochus IV, surnamed Epiphanes, or the "God
Manifest," in 164 B.C. that the storm broke in all its
fury. The forces then set in motion for the destruction
of the Seleucid empire were of two kinds, external and
internal. Of the external forces we have already considered one — the advance of the Roman power toward
the East. The Roman Senate had at this time only one
concern in its dealings with Syria, namely, to make the
Seleucids harmless. This it accomplished in a variety
of ways. Immediately after the death of Antiochus IV,
it sent commissioners into Syria who executed an unen-
forced article of the treaty struck after the battle of
Magnesia: they burnt the Seleucid battleships found in

the cities of Phœnicia and hamstrung the war elephants which they discovered in the royal arsenals. By jealously restricting the military establishment of the Seleucids the Senate broke their power in all respects. Not content, however, with binding the feet of its victim, the Senate held out an encouraging hand to all rebels against his authority. A case in point is that of the Jews. Again and again, between 164 and 120 B.C., Judas and Jonathan Maccabæus and Hyrcanus I sought and obtained Roman recognition in their struggle against their overlords. They had national causes for their repeated outbreaks and religious stimuli to resist desperately, but it is doubtful whether they could have carried their war of independence to a successful termination without the assurance that Rome sympathized with their enterprise. The Senate helped on the disruption of the Seleucid realm by still another unfriendly act: it joined with Pergamum and Egypt in lighting the fire of dynastic war in Syria in 153 B.C. and in adding fuel to it from time to time thereafter, with the result that the realm was devastated by civil war almost continuously from that date till the end of the dynasty, ninety years later. Then, the blackened hulk, manned by a mutinous crew, lay helpless in a sea infested with pirates, when Pompey picked it up and towed it into a Roman harbor.

The other external force which contributed to this inglorious end of a voyage begun with such fair promise was set in motion from the Farthest East. I do not reckon

it in this account that the Parthians again rebelled and
in 140 B.C. advanced their western frontier to the Euphrates, thus forming the philhellen kingdom of west
Iran which grew behind the breastwork of the Seleucid
empire to such power that later it disputed with some
success Rome's claim to suzerainty in Asia. Nor do I
enter it here that Armenia established its complete independence, and under Tigranes the Great annexed for
a time (83–69 B.C.) all of the Seleucid realm then remain-
ing. For these are internal movements analogous to the
insurrection of the Jews. It was from the banks of the
Hoang-Ho that an advance toward the west occurred
in the early part of the second century B.C. which may
be paralleled with the simultaneous advance eastward
of the Roman power from the banks of the Tiber.[1] The
oncoming Eastern assailant was the conglomerate of
Indo-European peoples whom the Chinese call the Yue
Tchi. They came along the edges of the great desert of
shifting sand in Eastern Turkestan down which flows the
mouthless Tarim River, not with the *élan* of conquerors, but retreating slowly before the superior strength
of the Huns (Hioung Nou), their former subjects, with
whom they had recently fought an unsuccessful war for
the possession of North China. It was against their
conquerors, we may remark in passing, that the Chinese
emperors, Chi-Houang-ti and Wou-ti of the Ts'in and

---

[1] Cordier, H., *Journal des Savants* (1907), pp. 247 *ff.*; Cunningham,
Numismatic Chronicle (1888), pp. 222 *ff.*

Han Dynasties respectively, constructed in the third and second centuries B.C., to the south of the Desert of Gobi, the great Chinese *Limes*, or Wall. In 159 B.C. the Yue Tchi occupied Sogdiana. Twenty years later (139 B.C.) they crushed the Greek kingdom of Bactria; so that in this general region it was only in India, in the vast district drained by the Indus River, that Greek kingdoms existed thereafter. Somewhere near the opening of the Christian era these, too, succumbed to the Yue Tchi, now properly designated Indo-Scythians by the Greeks. For several centuries the Indo-Scythians, like the Huns who followed them in the fifth century of our era, and the Turks who followed the Huns in the sixth, kept open the trade routes along which they had themselves advanced when driven westward from the Hoang-Ho. Their successors transmitted to the frontiers of China Manichæism, the cosmopolitan religion of Iran: *they* did a greater work. They not only forwarded Buddhism to the Chinese; but before it, and with it, the pure as well as the debased art of Greece. Among the priceless treasures which Dr. Stein has brought back from the desert cities of Cathay, none are more remarkable than certain clay seals attached to documents of the third century of our era, found at Niya in a district then under Chinese control; [1] for one of them might have been made for Diodotus, the first Greek king of Bactria, while on others appears Athena Alcis, the haughty,

[1] *Ruins of Desert Cathay* (1912), i, pp. 274, 284.

helmeted, *promachus* Athena, hurling the thunderbolt, whom the Antigonid kings of Macedon and the Greek kings of India had put on their coins.[1] Not without some reason, therefore, is the view now being advanced that the art of China and Japan is derived, like that of Europe and America, from Greek sources.[2] It is an amazing spectacle to observe how Hellenistic civilization flowed simultaneously back the channels to the springs in Italy and China whence came the floods which overwhelmed the Seleucid empire.

After this rapid survey of the political history of the Seleucids, I wish to devote the remainder of this chapter to considering the domestic policy of the dynasty. I shall point out that Seleucus and his successors continued Alexander the Great's work of founding city-states in Asia, and that, having to deal with priestly communities and feudal lords as well as with the occupants of the widespread royal domains, they refused to exempt from their direct control any lands not placed under the jurisdiction of a city-state. I shall discuss briefly the internal structure of the city-states and more at length their relation in theory and fact to the monarch. This will finally bring up for examination the policy of Antiochus IV, in whose reign the internal as

---

[1] W. W. Tarn, *Journal of Hellenic Studies*, XXII (1902), pp. 268 *ff.*, and *Antigonus Gonatas*, frontispiece; Gardner, P., *Numismatic Chronicle* (1887), p. 177.

[2] *Encyclopædia Britannica* [11], *s. v. Hellenism* (Bevan).

well as the external development of the Seleucid empire culminated.

Seleucus had been advanced to high position in Alexander's service after Alexander had disclosed his purpose of fusing the Macedonians, Greeks, and Iranians into a new cosmopolitan race. The promotion obtained by him during the course of the bitter struggle which this policy occasioned suggests that he made Alexander's point of view his own. This surmise as to the attitude of Seleucus is confirmed by the fact that he took his place, after Alexander's death, with those who upheld the cause of Alexander's family, and left it for his Babylonian satrapy only when it became clear that to remain meant to perish without accomplishing anything.

Seleucus was the only one of the great Macedonian captains who did not take Alexander's death as a license to discard their Iranian wives. The Bactrian maiden assigned to him at the great Susian marriage — Apama, daughter of Spitamenes — became his queen and the mother of his heir, Antiochus. The Seleucid dynasty was, accordingly, half Iranian from the start; and for the policy which it inherited from Antigonus and Alexander, and which it prosecuted vigorously till the death of Antiochus IV in 164 B.C., namely, the Hellenization of Asia, it had as warrant the practice of its idealized founder.

Of the Greek cities which Seleucus planted in his

realm, fifty-nine are named by Appian.[1] They lay especially in Syria, in the district between the Euphrates and the sea which he sought to make a second Macedonia. His son Antiochus, to whom he gave the administration of the eastern satrapies in 293 B.C., was particularly active in developing cities on the Greek model in that region; and to him and his son Antiochus Theos belongs the honor of establishing the urban habits of Hellenic life in the interior of Asia Minor. In the arm of their realm which reached through this peninsula to the rear of the Greek strip on the Anatolian coast, new cities sprang up under their auspices by the score. Nor did the movement come to an end with the reign of the second Antiochus in 246 B.C., though it probably weakened at that time. Over two generations later, in the reign of Antiochus IV, it was again resumed actively and directed especially into Palestine, which had been newly added to the realm.

The most striking feature in the internal policy of the Seleucids is the attempted transfer into Asia of the urban form of life theretofore characteristic of Hellas. Evidently, these monarchs believed with Aristotle, Alexander, and, we may add, Polybius, and, indeed, all Greeks, that men who did not live in cities were uncivilized men. Evidently, too, they thought it wise and possible to civilize their dominions.

It is not easy to form a definite impression of the

[1] *Syr.* 57; cf. Droysen, *Gesch. d. Hellenismus*², III, 2, pp. 254 *ff.*

political situation in the Seleucid realm when the Macedonians first took possession, but cities in the Greek sense seem to have been entirely absent. This does not mean that towns were lacking altogether, since, even if we disregard administrative centres like Babylon, Susa, Ecbatana, Persepolis, we may use the term "town" properly of places like Bambyce in Syria, fourteen miles west of the Euphrates. There, in a fertile, well-watered valley, stood a famous temple of Atargatis, the Syrian goddess. It was a wonderful establishment, as readers of Lucian know, with its wide approaches, its obelisk-like *phalli*, its sacred fish-pond, its shocking rites. At its head were emasculated priests, who not only conducted the ceremonies and directed a far-reaching proselytism, but also governed the community of temple slaves (*hieroduli*) who tilled the land of the neighborhood for their own support and that of the church. This clerical form of local organization had been carefully fostered by the Persians. We all know how in reorganizing Judæa they put the common people, who were there simply to pay tithes, under the control of the high priest, elders, and Levites, and made the so-called law of Moses the civil law of the land. They proceeded in similar fashion throughout Asia Minor. There Seleucus found scores of towns, big and little, to which the description, given by Strabo[1] of the sacred city of Ma at Comana in Cappa-

---

[1] XII, 2, 3, p. 535. Rostowzew, *Studien zur Geschichte des römischen Kolonates*, pp. 269 ff.

docia, is applicable: "In itself it is," he says, "a notable
city, but most of its inhabitants are god-possessed, or
temple slaves. They are all of Cataonian stock and are
subject generally to the authority of the king, but are
under the immediate control of the priest. He is lord
at once of the temple and of the temple slaves, of whom
there were more than six thousand, including men and
women, at the time of my visit. Attached to the temple
is much land, of which the priest enjoys the revenues,
and there is no one in Cappadocia of higher dignity
than he except the king." Similar to this was the temple
of Zeus at Venasa with its three thousand temple slaves
and its land which yielded to its priest an annual income
of twenty thousand dollars (fifteen talents); the temple
of Zeus Asbamæus near Tyana, of Apollo in Cataonia,
Mater Zizimene near Iconium, and Artemis Perasia in
Castabala. Similar, too, was the temple of Ma in Pontic
Comana with its swarming mart, its wide acres, and its
six thousand temple slaves, of whom the young women,
here as elsewhere, were sacred prostitutes; the temple
of Anaitis in Zela, of Men in Cabira, of Selene in Iberia,
of the Great Mother at Pessinus, of Zeus at Olba, and of
other gods in other places scattered through Phrygia,
Pisidia, and Lydia, as well as Palestine, Syria, and
Babylonia. The Seleucids must have found the body
of their empire thickly studded with religious communities, each subject to its own code of divine law, each
dominated by a masterful and long-petted theocracy.

Under this baleful rule the whole country had settled gradually down during the Persian time in progressive political and economic stagnation.

Apart from the mountains and the deserts, where tribal and nomadic liberty reigned, — a constant menace to central government, — the peoples of Asia lived in villages when the Macedonians came. Many of these villages, villagers and all, were owned by princelings and noblemen, who, if natives, had been undisturbed by the Persians, if Iranians, had come into their possessions by reason of royal grants. All through Syria and Asia Minor may be seen to-day the ruins of "square towers" (*tetrapyrgiæ*) and manorial castles such as these grandees built and fortified for defense against their neighbors and, if need be, against the royal authority itself.[1] Those who built them had apparently had little loyalty to the Persian king, but also little inclination to obey his successor. They were, accordingly, ejected right and left. Of the estates thus obtained, the Macedonian kings could dispose at their pleasure. They formed again part of the royal domain, which stretched in all directions at the edges of the deserts and the mountains, among the temple lands, the feudal fiefs, and administrative cities — a veritable archipelago of landed property, tilled for the crown by myriads of royal serfs. Here was the ὕλη, the material, of which the Seleucids founded many of their city-states.

[1] Butler, *Publications of an American Expedition to Syria*, II (1903), pp. 121 ff., 177; cf. Rostowzew, *op. cit.*, p. 254.

The handle for reorganization which the priestly towns offered to the new government was often the non-ecclesiastical part of the population. That the temple was regularly the centre of local trade and the scene of a recurrent bazaar tempted to its proximity money-changers and the like. When the Greek immigration began this element was naturally strengthened. It was, therefore, possible for the Seleucids to give it an urban organization — a general assembly, a council, and magistrates; and in this way to create a new city-state.

According to invariable Greek practice, however, such a city controlled — with certain limitations — its own shrines. The great temples of Apollo at Delphi and Delos, for example, were governed by the citizens of those towns. Hence the natural policy for the Seleucids, and the one which they in fact followed wherever practicable, was to subordinate the high priests and clergy to the adjacent urban authorities, thus solving the ecclesiastical question in a way convenient for themselves and agreeable to European feeling. Where this did not prove practicable, they often despoiled the temple of its lands for the benefit of their followers. Thus the village of Bætocæce was taken from the local temple of Zeus and given to a certain Demetrius, and the sacred land of Zeus of Æzani was divided into lots, which were assigned to cleruchs, subjected to a tax, and attached to the financial jurisdiction of an adjoining city.[1] It is simply

[1] Dittenberger, *Orientis Græcæ Inscriptiones Selectæ*, 262, 502.

another aspect of the same general policy when king after king sought to lay "impious" hands upon the treasures stored up in the temples of Bel, Anaitis, Atargatis, and Jehovah.

The secularization of religious properties was a very difficult matter, and it was not pushed at all times with equal vigor by the Seleucids. When the monarchs were embarrassed by foreign or domestic troubles, they had to conciliate the priests even to the point of undoing what they had already done. How easily a reaction might occur we can perceive from the case recorded in the splendid inscription which Mr. Butler has recently found cut on the inner wall of the great temple of Artemis at Sardis.[1] A certain Mnesimachus, presumably a Macedonian officer or adventurer, had got a huge fief from King Antigonus. It consisted of the village of Tobalmura in the Sardian plain and its appurtenances, the villages of Tandu and Combdilipia. On these he had to pay annual dues of £50 to the proper chiliarchy, or subdivision of the satrapy. Near by, in Cinara was a *kleros*, or lot, on which he paid £3 yearly. The fief consisted, in addition, of the village of Periasasostra, of which the annual dues, payable to another chiliarchy, were £57. Close by, in Nagrioa was again a *kleros*, on which he paid £3 7s. yearly. The fief consisted, moreover, of the village of Ilu in the territory of the well-

---

[1] Buckler and Robinson, *Greek Inscriptions from Sardis.* (*American Journal of Archæology*, XVI, 1912, pp. 11 ff.)

known city of Attuda, of which the dues, paid annually
to the city of course, were £3 5s. The manor (*aule*) of
the fief was in the village of Tobalmura, and together
with certain lodges held by bailiffs and certain gardens
and parks tilled by manorial serfs in Tobalmura and
Periasasostra, it had once been assigned to Pytheus and
Adrastus, likewise Macedonians; but later on it had
seemingly come into the possession of Mnesimachus.
The happy holder of this great estate enjoyed, doubtless,
the total net yield of the manor and the lots, and, in
addition, as the possessor of the manor and lots, rights
to exact services in money, kind, and labor from the
villeins of the villages. Had he been so minded he might
have settled down in Lydia and become a baron like
the Iranian nobles whom the Macedonians dispossessed; and, doubtless, many Macedonians and Greeks
established themselves in Asia in this fashion. Mnesimachus, however, wanted money rather than "rights";
and, turning to the temple of Artemis in Sardis, he secured a loan of £1325 from the temple treasurers. The
inscription cut on the temple wall records the sale to
Artemis, with right to repurchase, of Mnesimachus's
interest in the fief. His inability to repay his loan resulted in the aggrandizement of the temple.

Incidents of this sort were, doubtless, of frequent
occurrence and show what the Seleucids had to guard
against. Their land policy seems to have been prudent
and far-sighted. They were bound to deal cautiously with

their gigantic domain, since from it came the most valuable and stable portion of their revenues. On the other
hand, they found a limit set to the quantity which they
could profitably retain by the fact that, unlike the
Ptolemies, they inherited from the Persians a public
service adequate, not to administer, but simply to super-
vise administration. They did indeed increase the number of their satrapies, without, perhaps, diminishing the
number of chiliarchies or hyparchies into which each
satrapy was divided, and they seem to have paralleled
the general service by a distinct fiscal service and by a
distinct priestly service; but, none the less, they had to
leave the details of fiscal, judicial, and religious administration to the villages. Though we are singularly
ill-informed as to how they organized the villages, it is
conceivable that they picked out certain persons, like the
elders in the Egyptian villages, and held them responsible for the taxes of the villagers and for their general
good behavior. These men would be rather hostages
than officials, and would be nominees of the central
government rather than of the villages. But we really
know nothing of the facts, except that the villagers had
some means by which they paid their taxes collectively.

One way by which the Seleucids could relieve themselves of the troubles of local administration and at the
same time strengthen their hold upon the country was
to make grants of whole blocks or complexes of their
land, villages and villagers and all, to Macedonian and

Greek feudatories, like Mnesimachus, who of course became responsible for the dues owing to the crown. But the evils of this system had been discovered by the Persian kings when they found their vassals more unruly than the villages. Hence the Seleucids refused to give a clear title to those to whom they made grants of portions of the royal domain, and in the case of Mnesimachus the temple of Artemis, to which he sold his rights, had to secure itself in the contract against the loss which it might sustain should the king recall his grant. On the other hand, when the king sold outright parts of the domain, as he frequently did, particularly in times of financial distress, and the lands and villages sold became with their peasants private property, he required that they should be added to the territory of some city-state, it being a privilege highly cherished by the purchasers that they should be given the liberty of deciding to which city their property should belong. The Seleucid policy that land should belong either to a city-state or to the crown was admirably calculated to destroy priestly and feudal sovereignties, and it was taken over by the Roman emperors, into whose patrimony in Asia Minor passed many temple lands which had either escaped secularization under their predecessors or had been regained by the priests during the later, weaker days of the Seleucid dynasty.[1]

By a similar sale, or by a gift outright, the colonists

---

[1] Calder, *Classical Review*, XXVII (1913), pp. 9 *ff.*

who formed a new city, or the old inhabitants of a village on being constituted citizens of a free town, obtained full ownership of the lots of land assigned to them. The citizens, in turn, had authority, subject of course to the city's laws and the constitutions of the realm, over the serfs when there happened to be any on their holdings. In this way the king lost control of his peasants and his property; for the foundation was not merely a new city, but at the same time a new state. Its sovereign was not, or not simply, the king: it was the body of its franchised inhabitants assembled in general assembly, and it proceeded to manage its public affairs by means of discussion and resolutions, by delegating functions to a council and magistrates, and by determining its own domestic and foreign policies. The language of public life was of course Greek. The code of public and private law was, doubtless, drafted according to Hellenic models. Gymnasia appeared and with them gymnastic and musical contests — the most characteristic marks of Greek education. The deities they honored were those whom they themselves chose: they chose native gods and goddesses as well as Greek; above all they chose as their chief city-god the living emperor.

The Seleucid empire was a state without a citizenship. If an Athenian settled in it, he remained an Athenian, even if he became a satrap, unless he were given citizen rights in some one of the free cities. In other words, the empire had as many different citizenships as there were different cities, and as many distinct states as there were distinct citizenships.

Accordingly, each city could adopt whatever policy it pleased in the matter of admitting foreigners, be they Greeks or Asiatics, newcomers or natives, to its body politic. It might prohibit the intermarriage of citizens with non-citizens altogether, or it might go so far as to open its doors to bastards. It is, therefore, impossible for us, without such sources of knowledge as the papyri afford for Egypt, to speak in any general way of the extent and effects of racial fusion in the Seleucid empire. Two things, however, seem clear: (1) Intermarriage between citizens of different cities was of frequent occurrence and, doubtless, of full legal propriety; (2) the great mass of the agricultural population was not much affected racially by the proximity of Greeks, Macedonians, Jews, or Iranians. The peasants were practically serfs. Their social inferiority protected them against assimilation by citizens. On the other hand, they were, doubtless, much more deeply stirred by the European immigration than were the fellahs in Egypt; for the influx into their land was much more abundant and more spontaneous than was that into the valley of the Nile. Here, too, Hellenism had much more effective agents for its diffusion than it had there. For within the hundreds of city-states in Asia we must presume that intermarriage was permitted among all citizens, whether the elements which mingled with the Greeks were Phryg-

ians, Lydians, Syrians, Jews, Babylonians, or Iranians.
We must presume that at least the men knew in a
fashion the Greek language. They certainly tended to
take Greek names, and in documents of Delos dating
from the second century B.C. we meet with natives of
Bambyce — now a *polis* and renamed Hierapolis, or
the Sacred City — who would be indistinguishable from
native-born Greeks were it not for the Semitic names of
their wives. Indeed, some of them may have been
Greeks who had married Syrian women. The various
circles of Europeans in Syria, and, though to a less
degree, elsewhere in Asia, must have been surrounded
at an early date by a penumbra of half-breeds, by means
of which the sharp contrast of antagonistic civilizations
was lessened. In these circumstances Greek ideas and
customs became a ferment which stirred the peoples of
Asia to the depths. The awakening of the Nearer East
was in progress in the third century B.C., and had the
Romans succumbed to Hannibal and the Greeks maintained their prestige unimpaired for a century or two
longer, the whole course of history would have been
changed.

The Greeks came to Asia "not to send peace but a
sword." They came to fill the continent up with can-
tankerous little republics where formerly a dense multitude had lived in a state of political lethargy. And curiously enough those who directed the dismemberment of
Asia into far more states than even mediæval Germany

produced were the rulers who had the responsibility for
the government of the whole region. How explain this
anomaly?

The anomaly is more apparent than real. The ruler
was not simply the great landed proprietor of the cities'
neighborhood; he was the founder, or the descendant of
the heroized founder, of most of them; he was the "benefactor" or the "preserver" of them all. As such he was
deserving of their homage and entitled to their obedience.
This they could proffer in an unobjectionable manner
once Alexander had shown them the way. They had
simply to make their proskynesis; to elect him to membership in their circle of deities, furnish him with a
sacred precinct, temple, altar, image, procession, and
contest, and designate a priest to attend to the sacrifices
and other matters pertaining to his worship. This they
did of their own volition during the reign of the founder
of the dynasty. Apotheosis without territorial limitations Antiochus I demanded for Seleucus "after his
departure from the life among men," and the second
Antiochus demanded it for himself and his sister-wife
during their lifetime as well as for their "departed"
father; so that just as in Egypt and for the same reasons
an imperial cult of the rulers dead and living was established throughout not only the satrapies and hyparchies
but also the cities of the realm.[1]

---

[1] Kärst, *Gesch. des hellen. Zeitalters*, II, I, pp. 419 *ff.* Bouché-
Leclercq's treatment of this subject (*Hist. des Séleucides*, pp. 469 *ff.*), is
inadequate.

The city had, accordingly, a dual character: it was at once both in theory and fact a nation and a municipality. In the former capacity it could grant or withhold allegiance to the king; in the latter it had simply to obey. It had for example to pay tribute to him (*phoros* or *syntaxis*), which might be viewed as a rent for the land assigned to it, or as the price paid for military protection. It might have not simply a priest of the king and a priestess of the queen, but also a resident (*epistates*), who on occasion might also be *phrurarch*, or commandant, of the royal garrison when it had one. The double status of the city is further evidenced by the fact that its citizens were subject not only to the laws which they themselves passed but also to the mandates (*prostagmata*) which the king issued. In cases of conflict there could be no doubt which was superior. The king was in theory absolute as a god was absolute. He had, of course, citizenship in no state, but was simply *basileus*, or king. This title, attached to the name without an *ethnicum*, was the only one that the early Seleucids used; but the later members of the dynasty, beginning with Antiochus IV, added to it the title, such as Epiphanes, or God Manifest, by which their peculiar office as gods was indicated. Thereafter, on their coins and edicts the two titles appeared, and the monarchs were thereby classified in the two worlds to which they belonged — that of men and that of gods — as completely as were citizens when to their names were added the adjectival forms of their

city's name. In either capacity they were superior to
the cities. On the other hand, the Seleucid god-kings
had to consider carefully the demands of their cities,
since these, having the means to organize resistance,
could easily revolt. When they did not get satisfaction
they might choose some other god-king instead, as the
cities in Parthia and Bactria actually did; or they might
secure immunity from tribute, as did the cities in Asia
Minor in the reign of Antiochus I. Room was, accordingly, left for a large measure of municipal liberty; and,
in general, the activities of the citizens were numerous
and important. They had to attend to the maintenance
of order, the administration of justice, and the collection
of taxes within their several territories. Hence the cities
gave a stimulus to political interest and ambition such
as Asia had never known before. They occupied, in fact,
a place in the Seleucid empire quite as important as that
of the municipalities in the early Roman empire, of
which they were, indeed, the prototypes.

The Roman empire, however, had not yet come into
existence. It was the Italian federation under Rome's
leadership which defeated Hannibal and won the battles
of Thermopylæ and Magnesia. When compared with
this aggregate of incorporated and allied states, the Seleucid empire demonstrated fatal weaknesses. Rome had,
perhaps, not many more citizens on her army list than
there were males of military age in the franchised population of the Seleucid cities; and her public land, which,

too, was her chief source of revenue, was far inferior in extent and yield to the royal domain of the Seleucids. Her advantages were twofold and their enumeration will help us to understand the disabilities under which the Asiatic monarchy labored. First, apart from the soldiers on Rome's army list there were few males of military age in Italy; in other words, there was no vast native population to hold in subjection. Second, Rome could mobilize her forces much more easily, quickly, and completely than could the Seleucids. The great distances, often of mountain and desert, which separated the cities of Asia from one another; the considerable trading, industrial, Asiatic, and otherwise unwarlike, element in the free population of the Hellenic and Hellenized cities; and the independence of the cities, particularly in the matter of giving or refusing military aid to their suzerain, had no parallel in Italy, where the territory was compact, the population mainly a warlike peasantry, and the cities all bound to provide troops at the call of Rome to the full extent of their power. Like the giant Antæus in his trial of strength with Heracles, Rome with every fall renewed her might from contact with her native soil. The Seleucids ruled over a cosmopolitan, denationalized world. They had no native soil on which to fall. It is of profound significance that there were and could be no fellow-citizens of Seleucus in all Asia. The loyalty of true men in his realm was due first of all to their cities, and it was only by the lapse of time that a secondary loyalty to the ruling dynasty ceased to imply treason to their native states. The cities stood always before the decision whether in any given case they had more to gain or to lose by abandoning the Seleucid and transferring their allegiance to his enemy or to some other king.

It was the tragedy of Antiochus IV that through an education in Italy he came to realize fully the political grounds for the military superiority of Rome, and that through a sentimental attachment for Athens and the art, letters, and philosophy for which Athens stood, he renewed his conviction as to the absolute superiority of Greek culture.[1] He attempted to push more vigorously than ever the dynastic policy of Hellenization, by which alone a new nation could be bred in Asia, at a time when native hopes were revived; and he tried to draw the city-states of his realm into more complete dependence upon himself by the only means available to him — the right which he possessed as one of their gods to unhesitating obedience in all matters — at the very time when this policy came into collision with a religion to which deification of kings was an abomination. For in 200 B.C. Palestine had passed from the control of Egypt into the control of Antiochus the Great, whereupon his dynasty had to deal with the Jews. The trouble was, of course, that the Jews were monotheists. Many Jews in Jerusalem, as well as in the other cities of the

[1] *Hellenistic Athens*, pp. 303 *ff.*

realm, were not averse to Hellenism, and frequented
the gymnasia, enrolled their sons in the ephebe corps,
and gave them Greek names, but the devout shrank with
horror from worshiping the emperor, and the peasants
from everything foreign. Accordingly an open revolt
occurred in Judæa, chiefly among the country people,
when Antiochus IV chartered Jerusalem as a Hellenized
city, substituted for the bizarre law of Moses an enlightened, up-to-date, Greek code, and set down his own
image as the Olympian Zeus in the Holy of Holies.

This is the same Antiochus who twice led his victorious army to the walls of Alexandria, once to retreat after
dictating terms to the Ptolemies, once to meet a Roman
embassy headed by his old friend Gaius Popillius. Before answering the king's pleasant greeting, the Roman
handed to him the message of his Senate and curtly bade
him read it. He found it to be an order to evacuate
Egypt immediately. On asking for time to consider the
proposal, he got a further surprise; for, drawing a circle
round the king in the sand with his cane, Popillius demanded an answer "Yes" or "No" before he stepped
outside of it. A few months earlier, by crushing Perseus
of Macedon on the battle-field of Pydna (168 B.C.), Rome
had rid itself of its last serious rival. Since for Antiochus
to resist meant now to stand alone against the master
of the world, the only answer he could give was "Yes";
yet it meant the ruin of the Seleucid empire. Thereafter,
there was but one free will in the vast territory of Africa,

Asia, and Europe which lay between the Euphrates River
and the Atlantic Ocean — the will of the government
of Rome. Instruments to give it continuous effect in
Italy that sagacious and persistent corporation, the
Roman Senate, had made and used already; and in its
march to universal empire it had broken and hurled to
the ground the instruments of authority raised against it
by its Greek adversaries. To pick them up, mend them,
and improve them for further use was the imperial task
of the immediate future.

SELECT BIBLIOGRAPHY

1. SCHÜRER, E. *Geschichte des jüdischen Volks im Zeitalter Jesu Christi*, I[3] (1901), II[4] (1907).
2. BEVAN, E. *The House of Seleucus* (1902).
3. NIESE, B. *Geschichte der griechischen und makedonischen Staaten.* Especially Vol. III (1903).
4. BELOCH, J. *Griechische Geschichte*, III (1904).
5. ROSTOWZEW, M. *Studien zur Geschichte des römischen Kolonates* (1910), pp. 240 *ff.*
6. WILAMOWITZ-MOELLENDORFF, ULRICH VON. *Staat und Gesellschaft der Griechen : D. Die makedonischen Königreiche* (1910).
7. BOUCHÉ-LECLERCQ, A. *Histoire des Séleucides* (1913).

VII

THE EMPIRE OF THE ANTIGONIDS

OF the Hellenistic empires the one from which Rome suffered most and learned least was that of the Antigonids in Macedon and Greece. We say "Macedon and Greece": the kings of Macedon from Philip II to Perseus said "Hellas"; for they never ceased to claim that Macedon was a part of Hellas — *the* part of Hellas which had earned by the achievements of Philip II and Alexander the right of hegemony for its kings. It was an imperial nation for which its king, nobles, and commons had an intense loyalty and pride, but which stood in their thinking to Hellas as Virginia did to the United States in the *ante-bellum* days, or as Prussia does to Germany, rather than as Austria does to the Austro-Hungarian empire.

It taught the Romans least because it had least to teach them. The one thing in which the Macedonians were masterful was the art of war; yet in this the Romans by native accomplishment were their superiors. They invented the phalanx, but the phalanx succumbed to the legion. In the art of government the Antigonids were resourceful, but to lift up a jellyfish on a spear-point is an impossible task. Yet that is what they had to do in Hellas. The only lessons of government they could teach were lessons of failure; but that this is not to their discredit is shown by the inability of Rome itself to cope with the same situation till Hellas was dead and desiccated. They were sagacious enough to realize that for a people with the customs, piety, and bluntness of the Macedonians a kingship was best which, to speak with Aristotle, was a perpetual magistracy and not an absolute monarchy. Hence they were under no necessity to demand that the Macedonians worship them as gods, and the Macedonians, having inherited rights which no Antigonid dared to ignore,[1] were under no legal necessity to thrust divinity upon their rulers. Hence the Antigonids alone of the Hellenistic dynasties governed as men supported by their people's loyalty, and not as gods to whom all things were permitted. They, moreover, organized no official cult of their family in Hellas, for reasons which will appear later. It was not Macedon but Greece which took the proud Roman victor captive and bore the arts to rustic Latium. For the Macedonians remained themselves a rustic people, and added little or nothing to the poetry, painting, sculpture, architecture, and science of Hellas.[2] Their élite were rulers and officers, their commons farmers and soldiers. From the time Philip II came to the throne (359 B.C.) to the battle of Cynocephalæ (197 B.C.), it is impossible to find a

---

[1] Tarn, W. W., *Journal of Hellenic Studies*, XXIX (1909), pp. 269 *f.*; Beloch, *Griechische Geschichte*, III, 1, pp. 386 *f.*; *Hellenistic Athens*, p. 190.

[2] Mahaffy, *The Progress of Hellenism in Alexander's Empire* (1905), p. 32.

decade, and not easy to find half a one, during which the able-bodied men of Macedon were not called to the standards at least once either to defend their country against foreign attack or to march north, south, east, or west against their lord's enemies.[1] Their dead were to be found in every valley of Hellas, and their emigrants in every land of Asia; but theirs was a prolific race, so that, despite their many losses in the interval, they put 29,000 Macedonians in the field in the last struggle with Rome, or 2000 more than stood under the command of Alexander the Great when he had completed his arrangements for the conquest of Asia.

Rome suffered more from the Antigonids than from any other Hellenistic dynasty because it had there alone to do with a nation of veterans under arms. The Macedonians were, as has been said, an imperial people, loyal to their kings, and ambitious to maintain their ascendancy in the world. While at war with Rome — the wielder of armies 100,000 strong — they were assailed simultaneously by their Hellenic vassals and rivals and attacked or abandoned by their Macedonian kinsmen in Asia and Africa; yet they held out under the Antigonids, in the first struggle for eight years (212–205 B.C.), in the second for four (200–197 B.C.), in the third for still another four (171–168 B.C.); and even after one half of their men of military age had fallen at Pydna, and their

[1] Wilamowitz-Moellendorff, Ulrich von, *Staat und Gesellschaft der Griechen: D. Die makedonischen Königreiche*, pp. 139 ff.

last king had died in captivity and his only son as a clerk at Alba Fucens, their conquerors were so seriously disturbed by the "throbbings of their ancient loyalty" that the Senate had finally to place a Roman proconsul on the throne of the great Alexander (148 B.C.).

Though sprung from a Macedonian stock, the dynasty of the Antigonids was bred in Asia, and it was transplanted into Macedon only in its third generation. That came about in the following way. The first Antigonus was made ruler of Phrygia when Alexander the Great left Asia Minor in 333 B.C., and he was still in possession of that satrapy when his sovereign died ten years later. With Phrygia as a starting point and a nomination as commander-in-chief of the royal forces in Asia as a pretext, he planned and fought with such success in the next decade that in the spring of 312 B.C. he seemed destined to add Macedon to Asia, which he already possessed; and with it to support and not to oppose him, he counted on being able to master the whole of Alexander's empire. We have already seen why this project failed, and also how a later attempt to accomplish the same purpose cost him his life and his Asiatic realm. He may have been over-ambitious. Possibly no one could have prevented the dismemberment of the Græco-Macedonian world. Perhaps the centrifugal tendencies would have proved too strong for Alexander himself had he lived long enough to test them. That, however, does not make the issue less of a calamity for the Hellenes; for on the battle-fields of Gaza and Ipsus it was decided that the alien Romans and not the kindred Macedonians were to unite the world under a single government. With the person of the first Antigonus went to the grave the hope of a great people.

The sharer of his aspirations and the cause in considerable measure of his defeat was his son Demetrius, surnamed Poliorcetes, or "Taker-of-Cities." By his disobedience to orders at Gaza and his impetuosity in action at Ipsus, he had done most to lose his kingdom; but after the death of his father he still retained the dominion of the sea, and, with it, value as an ally and ability to use his forces at such points as he himself chose. After some years of aimless adventuring and galling inactivity he chose to use them in the attempt, twice vainly made already in coöperation with his father, to seize Greece and Macedon. His strength was incomparably inferior to that used on the earlier occasions and he had still watchful enemies on all sides. The essential difference was that the house of Antipater, which had ruled Macedon and Greece since Alexander the Great had crossed into Asia, was now represented, not by Antipater's able son, Cassander, who died in 297 B.C. after a reign of nineteen years, but by his weakly and dissentious children. These looked on inactive while he blockaded Athens (295–294 B.C.) and starved it into submission; whereupon he brushed them aside and took

their place as king of Macedon and suzerain of Greece.
Since his wife was Phila, Cassander's sister, his son, Antigonus, surnamed Gonatas, was a grandson of Antipater I, no less than Antipater II, who was now the sole
survivor of Cassander's family. Hence, if the right of
Demetrius Poliorcetes to the Macedonian throne rested
upon nothing more substantial than the frustrated ambition of his father, the right of his son was flawless after
the death of Antipater II. This, however, occurred in
288–287 B.C. at the very time when Demetrius, on
being expelled from Macedon, abandoned Greece and
went to meet captivity in Asia for the rest of his life.
Left behind in Greece, Antigonus Gonatas exercised a
watchful suzerainty there without being king of Macedon, which Pyrrhus of Epirus and Lysimachus of Thrace
shared for a few years (288 to 284–283 B.C.), Lysimachus,
Seleucus, and Ptolemy Ceraunus held alone in rapid
succession for another interval (283–280 B.C.), and Celts
from the north plundered and harried for three years.
It was not till 277 B.C. that Antigonus succeeded in free-
ing it from its troubles and making it the base of his
operations in Greece. He therewith planted in Europe
the dynasty which ruled Macedon till the Roman conquest (168 B.C.).

Antigonus I and Demetrius Poliorcetes had formed
their political ambitions and ideas during the age of the
diadochi, when the empire of Alexander stood in all its
magnificence and promise as a golden prize for the able,

courageous, and unscrupulous. They had aspired to rule as god-kings over a world in which men and cities rendered homage (proskynesis) to them, as they had rendered it to Alexander. They had viewed Greece and Macedon as alike desirable,[1] the common charm being that they were the mother of the soldiers and settlers of whom their limitless realm had need. They may have coveted Greece even more than Macedon. Certainly, Athens, not Pella, was the city of Demetrius's dreams. He had gloried in being its liberator in 307 B.C., and when it dashed his hopes by excluding him after his defeat at Ipsus, he had suffered bitter disappointment. None the less, and despite the desperate resistance which it had offered to him in 295–294 B.C., he treated it with clemency when he was once again its master. What his father had thought of the approval of Athens he expressed by calling it the beacon tower of the world. How highly he had esteemed the culture of its inhabitants he demonstrated by making a colony of Athenians the nucleus of Antigonia (later Antioch), which he founded as the new capital of the empire that had been Alexander's, but was now, he hoped, to be his.

Antigonus I had never had the good fortune to rule in the land of his birth, but Demetrius Poliorcetes was its king for six years (294–288 B.C.).[2] As such he showed

---

[1] For their revival of the Hellenic league, in which Macedon formed simply one unit, see Klotzsch, *Epirotische Geschichte*, p. 130, n. 1, and *Hellenistic Athens*, pp. 121 *f*.

[2] For the date see Mayer, *Philologus*, LXXI (1912), p. 227.

conclusively that he had no intention to reign there
patriarchally, as Cassander and Antipater, following
the example of Philip II and his predecessors, had done.
He displayed an utter disregard for the established customs of the court and for the limitations imposed by
usage upon his royal authority. The court he surrounded
himself with was the richly appointed, ceremonious,
uniformed affair devised by Alexander in his later,
more splendid, more arrogant days; and by requiring
proskynesis of the Macedonian noblemen and commons,
he offended, unnecessarily, as it proved, the sturdiest
sentiment of the nation.[1] His attempt to establish absolute monarchy in unsophisticated Macedon was the
most direct cause of the loss of his kingdom; for when
his foreign enemies, anticipating the attack which he
designed against them, assailed him from all sides, his
subjects hastened to abandon him and joined hands with
the invaders. They had no longer heart for the wild
imperialistic projects into which, almost without perceiving it, they had been led by Alexander the Great.

Antigonus Gonatas had never known the lure of the
East. He had spent his early manhood in Athens (294–
290 B.C.), where an unworthy liaison with the courtesan
Demo and an intimacy that does him honor with Zeno,
the founder of the Stoa, attest the range of his activity.
He won his spurs in his father's Bœotian campaigns of

[1] *Hellenistic Athens*, p. 148.

292–291 B.C., and spent the formative years of his career as a general and statesman in Greece (288–280 B.C.). Only once, when hard pushed in 280 B.C., did he show that the blood of Demetrius Poliorcetes and Antigonus I flowed in his veins, namely, when he tried to seize Asia Minor, then temporarily without a master. Normally, he acted like the child of Phila and the heir of the policy of Cassander and Antipater. And it was in the spirit of his mother's line that he established his government in Macedon on expelling the Celts in 277 B.C.

His reign opened auspiciously. Having obtained—how, when, and at what price, we do not know—the friendship of Egypt, he got the opportunity to order affairs to his liking in Greece. On the other hand, his accession to the throne was accompanied by his marriage to Phila, his own niece, the sister of Antiochus I, the new king of Asia. This union sanctioned an agreement by which Antigonus abandoned his claim to Asia Minor and Antiochus his right, as Seleucus's son, to the Macedonian throne. It inaugurated a policy by which Macedon secured for eighty years (277–197 B.C.) immunity from attack or intrigue on the part of the Seleucids. His friendship with Egypt was less enduring, but it gave him ten years (277–267 B.C.) in which to consolidate his power — a period of quiet activity, interrupted only by the return of Pyrrhus from Italy and the startling upheaval in Macedon and Greece (274–272 B.C.) which accompanied that adventurous monarch's vigorous as-

sertion of his right to rule those countries. The fall of
Pyrrhus in battle at Argos relieved the tension of this
situation, but till the time of his death thirty-two years
afterwards, Antigonus had always to count Epirus
among his possible enemies when it was not actually
his assailant. On his northern frontier he faced the
threatening Dardanians, and on the northeastern the
marauding Celts, who had reduced Thrace to the condition of barbarity that prevailed throughout Central
Europe. By keeping these peoples in check he did a
great service to Greece, which he thereby protected;
but for it he got little gratitude, and it was his suzerainty over Greece which brought to him and his successors most of their many troubles.

Just as he was faithful to the traditional policy of the
Macedonian kings in his dealings with his own people,
so, too, in regard to the Greeks the plan he followed was
in general the old-fashioned one, of making them his
dependent allies. In states ostensibly free and self-
governing he secured a preponderating influence by
designating an individual as his representative and
making him practically governor. Naturally, the domestic opponents of such a person called him a tyrant, and
such, in fact, the nature of his position forced him to
become, since he could not hold his place without break-
ing both the public and private laws. But outward
appearances were preserved, even when he called in
Macedonian troops to his aid, by the old practice

whereby he and his adherents assumed the responsibility for their coming.

Antigonus Gonatas and some at least of his governors were pupils of Zeno. That meant in this connection that, whereas Alexander the Great, for example, had been obliged to discard what was most characteristic in the politics of Aristotle when he identified himself with the man of transcendent virtue, who, his teacher had urged, should be made absolute monarch when found, Antigonus drew from his philosophy an obligation to let none but the sage rule.[1] As against the wisdom of the ideal wise man the laws of states which he ignored or broke had no avail; for, according to his creed, they were unnatural and hence unwholesome. The wise man could do no wrong. In his actions, since he was a law unto himself, morality triumphed over mere legality. Antigonus Gonatas disdained to seek a justification for his acts by claiming, though a man, the prerogatives of the gods, and, though there was nothing in the pantheistic theory of Stoicism to prevent his being worshiped if people wanted to worship him, he was under no legal necessity to pose as a god; whereas, had he done so, he must have come into conflict with the religious conservatism of his philosophy. He, accordingly, had no difficulty in rendering an account to his own conscience

---

[1] Wilamowitz-Moellendorff, *Antigonos von Karystos*, p. 218; Kärst, *Geschichte des hellenistischen Zeitalters*, II, 1, pp. 121, 125. Tarn (*Antigonus Gonatas*, pp. 276 ff.) bases Antigonus's system of tyrants on expediency, not on philosophy.

for setting up "tyrants" in his Greek dependencies and for practicing or authorizing lawlessness. But he was too shrewd a man to suppose that because Zeno and he thought his conduct justified he could do what he pleased to the Macedonians or Greeks with impunity. They could not be expected to know that their ruler was a Stoic sage who could do no wrong, or to make allowances for his behavior on that account. Hence, while he could justify his system of government on philosophic grounds, there is no evidence that he was not a scrupulous Macedonian king and a considerate suzerain of Greece. And had he been left alone to work out the problem of Hellenic administration without outside interference it is probable that his high sense of duty and his skill and forbearance would have given Greece a long period of peace.

The founder of the first Macedonian empire, Philip II, had been opposed in Greece by Persia, but the resistance he had encountered because of the diplomacy of Artaxerxes Ochus was as nothing when compared with the difficulties raised up for Antigonus Gonatas's uncle, Cassander, by the promises and armies of his grandfather, Antigonus I, or with the obstacles he himself had to meet in the intrigue, money, and expeditions of Ptolemy Philadelphus.

The situation which existed in the first ten years of his reign (277–267 B.C) was not of Antigonus's creating, nor was Philadelphus responsible for it. It was Ptolemy I

Soter who had seized the dominion of the sea on the final *débâcle* of Demetrius Poliorcetes (287–286 B.C.) and with it the control of the league of the Islanders. This established a long and, in fact, indefinable frontier between the realm of Philadelphus and that of Antigonus. The lordship of the sea Gonatas seems not to have bothered about at first, and, indeed, the great war which broke out in 266–265 B.C. between the two monarchs — the so-called Chremonidean War — was clearly incited by Egypt and not by him. Notwithstanding that she was dead four years when the actual conflict began, its real instigator was, doubtless, Arsinoë, the sister-queen of Philadelphus. Acting on her policy, Philadelphus first formed an alliance with King Areus I of Sparta and his allies (Achæa, Elis, Mantinea, Phlius, and part of Crete) and with Athens, and then backed them up in the concerted effort they decided to make to free Greece from Antigonus and his "tyrants." What the real object of the "brother-gods" was, is a matter of conjecture. All they accomplished, in any case, was to give Antigonus five years of hard fighting [1] and to complete the ruin of Athens and the enforced quietude of Sparta.

Therewith was accomplished, what had been long in the preparing, the overthrow of the leadership which city-states had held from time immemorial in European

[1] For the peace between Egypt and Macedon made in 261 B.C. see *Inscriptiones Græcæ*, XI, 2, 114.

Greece. Henceforth it was not from cities that significant movements sprang, but from ethne. Macedon itself was an ethnos, or, at least, a group of ethne, and it
seemed possible to enlarge it by adding to it all the other
ethne in the peninsula. The difficulty was that two
other ethne, Ætolia and Achæa, the first in Central
Greece and the second in the Peloponnesus, had each a
similar, if less far-reaching, ambition; and while the
aspirations of Ætolia to acquire territory in the Peloponnesus, and the aspirations of Achæa to expand into
Central Greece, kept them normally in conflict with one
another; and while each in turn (Ætolia in 245–241,
Achæa in 220–217 and 212–206 B.C) got the help of
Macedon against the other, and both united only once
(238–229 B.C.) in a war against Macedon, Achæa offered
till 224 B.C. and Ætolia till 200 B.C. an attractive alternative for Macedonian suzerainty to ethne and city-
states which could not stand alone. The natural desire
of the new ethne, as of the old city-states, was, however,
to be independent — a sentiment which Ætolia and
Achæa shared completely; and against this powerful
force Antigonus had to contend, after the Chremonidean
War no less than before it.

He had come so brilliantly out of the Chremonidean
War, however, that ten years elapsed before his suzerainty was again challenged. His most formidable
enemy, Ptolemy Philadelphus, was absorbed meanwhile
with a dangerous disturbance in Ionia, occasioned by

the revolt of Ptolemy, his "son", and Timarchus, his admiral, to whose aid his watchful enemy, Antiochus II, and his daring maritime rivals, the Rhodians,[1] had come (258 B.C.); but when this outbreak was brought to a close with the peace of 255 B.C.,[2] Antigonus had to anticipate a renewal of his troubles in Greece. He, accordingly, determined to cease being the anvil and to become the hammer. That meant the construction of a fleet with which to take from Egypt control of the Ægean, which had been possessed prior to 288–287 B.C. by his father and grandfather. To accomplish this end he renewed his alliance with Syria, and arranged a marriage between his son and heir, Demetrius, and Stratonice, Antiochus's sister. This being done, he sought out the admirals of Ptolemy at Leucolla near Cos, and defeated them in a great naval battle (253 B.C.). Suzerainty over the league of the Islanders was the most striking gain; but a more substantial advantage was that with his fleet he could now ward off trouble in Greece and stir it up in Ptolemy's realm. The latter he accomplished by dispatching his half-brother, Demetrius the Fair, to Cyrene and by snatching that kingdom, which had just been vacated by the death of Magas (251–250 B.C.), from

[1] The enmity of Rhodes and Philadelphus is proved by Blinkenberg's *La chronique du temple Lindien*. It is, accordingly, probable that the defeat of Chremonides by Agathostratus at Ephesus belongs to this struggle, though something may still be said, I think, for 242 B.C. See *Hellenistic Athens*, p. 197, n. 2.

[2] For this peace see *Inscriptiones Græcæ*, XI, 2, 116. Its effect is perceptible in Athens (*Hellenistic Athens*, p. 191) and in Achæa (*Ibid.*, n. 1).

the grasp of Egypt. In the former he had a rather surprising lack of success. For in 251 B.C. Aratus, the somewhat melodramatic hero of the Achæan league, on mastering his native city Sicyon by a coup d'état, not only chose to accept a subsidy from Philadelphus rather than from himself, but added Sicyon to the neighboring ethnos of the Achæans. And almost immediately thereafter Ptolemy struck a second blow which made the first of importance. In 250 B.C. Alexander, Antigonus's nephew and chief lieutenant in Greece, egged on by Egypt doubtless, revolted and set himself up as an independent monarch, with Corinth and Calchis, which he had held for his uncle, and the Macedonian fleet of which these were the naval stations, as his basis for action. He at once allied himself with the Achæans and forced Argos and Athens to pay him tribute (before 250–249 B.C.). This rebellion paralyzed the naval power of Antigonus. It was doubtless precipitated by the disloyalty of Antiochus II to Macedon; for that monarch (now, in or before 249 B.C.) broke faith with Antigonus and allied himself with Egypt, retaining the conquests he had made during the war and receiving in marriage Berenice, the only daughter of Philadelphus, whose intrinsic worth was augmented by an enormous dowry. This base and, as it proved, foolish action freed Ptolemy to devote all his energies to the war with Macedon. The fleet of Egypt once more mastered the Ægean and regained control of the league of the Islanders (249 B.C.). Simultaneously, the pro-Egyptian party in Cyrene slew the fair Demetrius, and by the marriage of their young queen Berenice to Philadelphus's heir, effected the reunion of the two kingdoms, which had been estranged since the revolt of Berenice's father, Magas, in 274 B.C.[1] The triumph of Ptolemy was complete, and when his daughter promptly bore to her Seleucid husband a son, who by the marriage stipulation was to be his heir, the future of the Ptolemies seemed bright indeed.

Between 250 and 245 B.C. the fortunes of Gonatas were at a low ebb. He evidently bent before the storm, unable to confront Alexander and Aratus in Greece and the admirals of Philadelphus in the Ægean. Relief came to him from an unexpected source — the renewal of the war between Egypt and Asia, when, on the death of Antiochus II, his sister-wife Laodice took up arms against the Egyptian queen and her babe on behalf of her son Seleucus Callinicus. For, helped by the untimely death of Philadelphus, and despite the intervention of the Egyptian fleet, she succeeded in compassing the death of her rivals;[2] whereupon the new Ptolemy, Euergetes, took the field in person and made a general

---

[1] Tarn (*Antigonus Gonatas*, pp. 321 *ff.*, 449 *ff.*) has Demetrius slain in 258 B.C., and Berenice married to Euergetes, in 247–246 B.C. This position, which Beloch challenged (*Griech. Gesch.*, III, 2, pp. 133 *ff.*), leaves unexplained the extraordinary delay in the marriage of the young couple and in the reunion of the two kingdoms.

[2] De Sanctis, *Contributi alla Storia dell' Impero Seleucidico* (*Atti della Reale Accademia delle Scienze di Torino*, XLVII, pp. 11 *ff.*).

attack by land and sea upon her and her adherents.
This tragic incident was one of the few pieces of good
luck experienced by Antigonus. Another was the pre-
mature death of his nephew Alexander (246 B.C.), followed as it was by the Ætolian conquest of Bœotia,
and the decision of Nicæa, Alexander's widow, to surrender Corinth and the rest of her kingdom to Macedon,
the arrangement being that she was to take the place
of the barren and discredited Stratonice as wife of the
crown prince Demetrius. In 245–244 B.C. the balance
in Asia inclined sharply in favor of Laodice, and at the
same time Antigonus, aided by his patron god Pan,
recovered Delos and the Islands. Having thus regained
what the rebellion of Alexander had cost him, and having settled his account with Egypt, Antigonus had now
to deal with Aratus of Sicyon alone. The Achæan was
too quick for him, however. By a night attack, in time
of peace, he treacherously seized Corinth (243 B.C.), and
at once added it, together with Megara, Epidaurus, and
Troezen, to the Achæan league. The response of Antigonus to this audacious coup was to form a pact with
his old friends the Ætolians to divide Achæan territory
between them; whereupon, as the only escape from so
great a peril, Aratus put the responsibility where the
responsibility really belonged, by having Ptolemy Euergetes elected general of the Achæan league on land and
sea for 242 B.C. Euergetes brought the Laodicean War
to a point where an advantageous peace was possible by

a victory over Callinicus in this critical year; but his attempt to help Aratus, who tried to "liberate" Athens while his "commander" engaged Gonatas in the Ægean, was frustrated by the defeat sustained by his admiral Sophron at the hands of the veteran Antigonus off the island of Andros. Macedon still held the Ægean. In the mean time its allies the Ætolians, already dangerously strengthened by the occupation of Bœotia, had worsted Olympias, the queen regent of Epirus, in several engagements, and were on the point of incorporating all of Acarnania in their league. Antigonus thought the time had come to call a halt. Euergetes and Callinicus were of the same mind. Accordingly, the long war was concluded in 242–241 B.C. by a general peace arranged on the basis of *uti possidetis*. Antigonus held Argos, Hermione, Phlius, Ægina, Megalopolis, and Orchomenus in the Peloponnesus, in Central Greece Athens alone, and in the Ægean Eubœa and the Cyclades, as well, seemingly, as Lemnos, Imbros, and Scyros, the colonies of Athens. Thessaly was of course his. His garrisons stood in Demetrias, Chalcis, and Piræus. Of the "shackles" of Greece Corinth alone was out of his hands. In 240–239 B.C. he died at the age of eighty, having been a king forty-seven years, all but ten of them in Macedon.

I have sketched the career of Antigonus Gonatas in some fullness chiefly because it has only recently become possible to give anything like chronological precision to an account of this remarkable man.[1] His reign deserves detailed consideration, however, because of the position it occupies at one of the culminating points of Greek imperialism, the only other point of equal importance being that in which Alexander the Great introduced deification of rulers. The record given above shows clearly, I think, that the power of Macedon did not suffice to hold Greece in subjection on the principles followed by Antigonus Gonatas, and against the opposition of Egypt. Even the final triumph of 242–241 B.C. left Egyptian garrisons in Thrace, the Hellespont, Ionia, and islands as far advanced into the Ægean as Thera and Astypalæa, Samos and Lesbos, Thasos and Samothrace. It left Achæa in possession of Corinth and Megara, Epidaurus and Troezen, as well as Sicyon and at least a foothold in Arcadia. It left Ætolia in possession of part of Acarnania, Dolopia, Æniania, Malis, Doris, Locris, Phocis, and in close alliance with Bœotia. Heraclea at Thermopylæ and Delphi with its Amphictyonic council were Ætolian. Hence when the new king of Macedon, Demetrius II, married Olympias's daughter Phthia, and took Epirote Acarnania under his

---

[1] The account given in the text differs from that given in *Hellenistic Athens* mainly because (led by Dürrbach, *Inscriptiones Græcæ*, XI, 2, pp. vi *f.* and Pozzi, *op. cit.* in Select Bibliography at the end of the chapter) I now return to Homolle's Delian chronology. It differs only in a few details from that given by Pozzi. Tarn's masterly biography (*Antigonus Gonatas*) reached me only when this chapter was already in type. The complete data which it contains agree well, I believe, with the construction given above.

protection (240-239 B.C.); and when Ætolia, thus check-
mated, entered into a defensive and offensive alliance
with Achæa, the territory of the two leagues, now united
in opposition to Macedon, met, and inclosed completely
the Corinthian Gulf. The one had grown strong despite
Antigonus and the other with his connivance. He had
been forced to give Ætolia a free rein from need of its
aid against Egypt, Epirus, and Achæa. Now the policy
of Epirus was subservient to that of Macedon as it had
been prior to the accession of Pyrrhus to its throne in
295 B.C., but the two leagues were able to fight on fair
terms with the two monarchies, and in 238 B.C. they de-
fied Macedon, now supported by Epirus, without having Egypt as their ally. The failure of the Greek policy
of Antigonus Gonatas may be best gauged by the fact
that twenty-seven years earlier Athens and Sparta had
dared to do the like, but only when Egypt, and probably also Epirus, were fighting on their side.

The chief reason for this striking difference is that in
the interval the Achæans, following the lead given to
them by the Ætolians, had come to life and shed their
ethnic cocoon. They had long since been a *koinon*, or
league; but up to 251 B.C. their league, like that of
Bœotia prior to 387 B.C., like that of the Ætolians prior
to the seizure of Delphi in 292 B.C., had been confined
strictly by the limits of their ethnos. The Ætolians had
enlarged their territory under the ægis of the Delphian
Amphictyony. The Achæans had no such favoring

circumstance. In their case expansion by the incorpora-
tion of "foreign" peoples was the policy and achievement of a citizen of the first "foreign" city to be
absorbed, Aratus of Sicyon, who saw a greater opportunity for power as the head of the neighboring league
than as the "tyrant" of his native state, holding office,
like the priest at Nemi, till murdered, or till he had lost
the confidence of Antigonus. At his instigation the
Achæan league was carried into the territory of the
"foreigner," the necessary prerequisite for such a
development being, however, that the ethnic bond
between the Achæan cities had been canceled and replaced by a federal bond. The tenacious theory that
common citizenship presupposed community of descent
was therewith discarded. Its abandonment opened to
the league possibilities of growth never possessed by
either the city-state or the ethnic state. Of these the
Ætolians and the Achæans took advantage to the best of
their abilities.

They were wise enough, moreover, to perceive that
not only were city institutions indispensable for an up-
to-date polity — whence the Ætolians on forming their
league in 322–314 B.C. abandoned their three ancient
tribes and their multitudinous villages and organized
in their stead a score or two of cities [1] — but also that
their federal system must recognize and accept the pre-

---

[1] Swoboda, *Die ätolische Komenverfassung* (*Wiener Studien*, XXXIV,
1912, pp. 37 *ff.*).

existent city-states as its units. This, as we have seen,[1] had not been done in Bœotia or in the Hellenic league organized by Philip II, in each of which the federal synod, being constructed on the idea of representation according to population, made districts and not cities the units; so that the smaller cities felt themselves discriminated against and tended to rebel against being clubbed together. How far equality of cities prevailed among the Achæans it is impossible to say with certainty: we are simply informed that the voting there was by cities. But we are, I think, permitted to infer that the principle followed was "one city one vote." For it is unlikely that the old Achæan cities, on admitting Sicyon, Corinth, Megalopolis, and Argos, deliberately exposed themselves to the fate of the little lake cities in Bœotia by giving these large "foreign" cities voting power proportionate to their populations. This conclusion holds, I believe, both for the Achæan representative assembly, or synod, which was made up, seemingly, of successive fractions of the citizens of the constituent cities,[2] and for the Achæan primary assembly, or *syncletus*, which was open to all citizens over thirty years of age. It holds, too, it seems, for the two Ætolian assemblies, the ordinary and the extraordinary, which were both primary,[3] but not for the Ætolian council

---

[1] Above, chapter I.

[2] De Sanctis, *Rivista di Filol.* XXXVI (1908), pp. 252 *ff*.

[3] Swoboda, *Studien zu den griechischen Bünden*, I (*Klio*, XI, 1911, pp. 456 *ff*.).

which was constituted of delegates apportioned to the constituent cities according to their size. The Achæan and the Ætolian leagues represent in this respect a reaction from the earlier leagues. Their hope was to change the stress of the cities, which came into play, from a centrifugal into a centripetal force by basing their federations squarely on the city-states.

This they could do, up to a certain point, the more easily because each ethnos had lacked a city-state of outstanding political and economic power. Equality of city-states did not conflict flagrantly with realities in either Achæa or Ætolia. Hence the principle that each city-state, irrespective of strength in the Aristotelian sense, should have a single vote in the federal assembly, and an equal voice in the choosing of the federal cabinet (*demiurgi; apocleti*), and the federal executive (*strategus*, hipparch, secretary of state, treasurer or treasurers) appeared equitable. In Bœotia and Hellas in the earlier time the league had been created by the superior strength of Thebes and Macedon respectively; and these capital states had taken care that the initial leadership should be preserved by the institutions of the leagues. The Achæan and the Ætolian leagues, on the other hand, were partly, no doubt, the result of a compromise between the constituent units, but mainly the consequence of foreign pressure. The federal movement was not based primarily upon the activity of any one city, but upon a need generally felt. Hence the capital of the

Achæan league was Ægium, and the capital of the
Ætolian league Thermon — neutral meeting-places, like
Washington, Ottawa, and Canberra. That was some-
thing new in the annals of the Greek leagues.

The creative force of foreign policy is manifest in still
other characteristics of these Hellenistic leagues. It was
almost inevitable that in those days of executive efficiency states should be monarchically organized. Hence,
whereas there had been eleven Bœotarchs in the Bœotian league and seven generals in early third-century
Acarnania, a single general stood at the head of the
Ætolians from the founding of their league and at the
head of the Achæans after 255 B.C. That gave a unity
of action otherwise impossible, the lack of which, though
negligible perhaps in domestic affairs, had been found
disadvantageous in foreign affairs. It was a necessary
concession to a monarchical age, one which, however,
had been made reluctantly and with an important
reservation which took from the serum its malignancy:
the generalship could be held by the same individual
only every alternate year. He might be the uncrowned
king of the league one year; the next he must be a private citizen.

In still another respect distrust of monarchy and aversion to the "tyranny" on which Antigonus Gonatas had
based his Greek empire, are betrayed in the institutions
of the Achæans. The rule of a city by a tyrant and
membership in the league were regarded as incompatible

with one another. This was, doubtless, a requirement of the federal laws, which, consisting of treaties negotiated between the original cities in 275 B.C. and at the admission of new cities thereafter, of oaths by which these treaties were sanctioned, and of general enactments made from time to time by special legislative process, bound the citizens of the individual cities no less than did the local laws which they themselves passed. Otherwise the city-states were at liberty to adopt whatever form of government they chose. The league championed neither democracy nor oligarchy, though its working favored the well-to-do classes. At most it compelled a certain uniformity in local administration, its general attitude being admirably symbolized by its monetary arrangements, wherein the standard was determined by the federal authority while the coins were issued by the constituent cities.[1]

The very constitutions of the Achæan and the Ætolian leagues disclose the importance of the part which the Greek policy of Antigonus Gonatas played in the creation of these dangerous adversaries of himself and his country. It is true that his son, Demetrius II, fought them to a standstill, wrested from Ætolia a large part of its acquisitions, and might have dissolved both leagues by force, had not Epirus deserted him and gone over

---

[1] Swoboda, *Studien zu den griechischen Bünden*, II. *Die Städte im achäischen Bünde* (*Klio*, XII, 1912, pp. 17 *ff.*).

to their side; had not the Illyrian pirates whom he let
loose on this new enemy provoked the Romans to cross
the Adriatic; and had not the Dardanians moved down
on Macedon and defeated and killed him in battle.
Such "had nots" belonged, however, to the constant
possibilities, and complications of this sort were ever
occurring in the struggle of Macedon for the hegemony
of Greece. On this occasion their issue was so disastrous
for Macedon that the hour of the two leagues seemed
come.

But what should have been their triumph proved
to be their destruction. For the frustration of their
hopes Polybius,[1] who voices the opinion of Aratus, held
the Ætolians responsible, and it is likely that he was
in the main right. For just at this critical moment, when
the Achæans were face to face with the most serious
problem which their federal system presented, namely,
the reluctance of states, like Sparta and Athens, which
were markedly stronger than the common run of the
Achæan cities, to accept mere equality with them, the
Ætolians not only left them in the lurch and made an
advantageous peace for themselves with Antigonus
Doson, the new king of Macedon, but, by ceding to
Sparta their Arcadian cities (Tegea, Mantinea, Orchomenus, and Caphiæ), they made it possible for Cleomenes, the young Spartan monarch, to rally round himself all the Peloponnesian opposition to the Achæans,

[1] II, 45.

and to make a brilliant effort to establish once again the Spartan hegemony in the peninsula. Another view of the matter is that the downfall of the Achæan league — which, to escape Cleomenes, threw itself into the arms of Antigonus Doson — was due to the intervention of Ptolemy III, who backed up Sparta, Athens, and Ætolia by his friendship and his money,[1] and would have gladly seen Achæa eliminated in order that Greece might present a united front to Antigonus Doson. In any case it was Antigonus Doson who reaped the benefits, and it seems unlikely that they were wholly an unearned increment. What he was capable of he had already shown by joining heartily in the international guarantee of the neutrality of Athens which had robbed Aratus of that choice prize. He was clearly no common man, and had he not died an untimely death shortly after the great victory he gained over Cleomenes at Sellasia (222 B.C.), he would probably have been much better known in history. His energetic and tactful conduct in this crisis contrasts sharply with the nerveless backdown of Egypt, for which the only excuse was the imminent demise of Euergetes and the threatening attitude of Antiochus the Great. It cannot be denied that Antigonus Doson made a good use of all his opportunities.

His settlement of Hellenic affairs was characterized by the revival of the general synod established by the great Philip.[2] Representatives of the Hellenic states met

[1] *Hellenistic Athens*, pp. 240 f.
[2] Freeman, *History of Federal Government*, pp. 379 ff.

in formal assembly at Corinth (224 B.C.), and chose the king of Macedon as their hegemon. Subsequently the synod was to meet at a time and place to be designated by its head. A mere enumeration of the states which took this action tells the story of the constitutional development of Hellas in the Macedonian age. They were Macedon, Thessaly, Epirus, Acarnania, Locris, Phocis, Bœotia, Eubœa, Achæa, and probably the Islanders. Of these the first was a kingdom,[1] but all the others were leagues. The city-states, which had been everything in Philip's synod, have disappeared, swallowed up in the federations. Whether each of the units had now an equal number of votes, or, as in the time of Philip, a number proportionate to its size, we do not know, though the second alternative is the more probable one. In both cases Macedonian deputies took part in the meetings of the synod and served as heads of the Macedonian interest. Together with the deputies from Thessaly and other subservient states they probably formed a majority in the synod. In both Philip II and Antigonus Doson, Macedon had, accordingly, at once hegemons and kings. We hear of nothing in the revived Hellenic league comparable with the Committee of Public Safety of the old one; but nothing similar was now required, since the generals of the constituent leagues were the natural representatives of these bodies when the synod was not in session. They

[1] And in all probability, a league as well. Tarn, *Antigonus Gonatas*, p. 54, n. 36.

had thus a place provided for them in the scheme of
Antigonus Doson.

The republican reaction against the policy of Antigonus Gonatas had by no means spent its force. This is
shown in the seriousness with which it was now reckoned
with by Antigonus Doson. He could not ignore the well
established practice of the league assemblies to decide
all important questions of foreign policy. Hence his synod
differs from that of Philip II particularly in this important respect, that its action in declaring war, concluding
peace, and other like matters was taken subject to rati-
fication by the league authorities, and was, seemingly,
binding only on such of them as ratified it.[1] His synod,
in other words, stood to the league assemblies as the
Achæan synod stood to the Achæan *syncletus*. Naturally,
the confederates could not withdraw from the hegemony
at pleasure, much less join its enemies; so that the refusal of a league to accept a decision of the synod to
declare war meant only that it assumed a position of
neutrality. In Philip's time each city had had to pay
per day a fine of thirty drachmæ for every horseman,
twenty drachmæ for every hoplite, ten drachmæ for
every light-armed soldier, and seven or eight drachmæ
for every sailor who was absent from a duly authorized
expedition.[2] Now the leagues could refuse to coöperate without suffering any penalty. They surrendered
their liberty to fight one another, and their right to

[1] Polybius, IV, 26.   [2] Wilhelm, *Attische Urkunden*, I, p. 36.

contract alliances with outside states; but they did not surrender their diplomacy entirely to the hegemon, though they agreed to enter into no negotiations with any outside king.[1] They gave their hegemon no right whatever to interfere in their local concerns.[2]

Such were the generous concessions to local sentiment by means of which Antigonus Doson sought to place the hegemony of the kings of Macedon in Hellas on a secure basis. Never before in the history of the people had a conqueror made so noble a use of his power. Antigonus Doson went in fact so far in conciliating the Greek states that had he withdrawn Macedonian troops from Demetrias, Chalcis, and Corinth, — the three shackles of Hellas, — added new conquests like Orchomenus, Sparta, and Messene to the constituent leagues instead of to the central organization, and possessed less personal prestige, it is difficult to imagine how the Hellenic league could ever have been brought into action. Probably all that he cared to be absolutely sure of was the neutrality of the confederates who did not support him in the field.

In any case that was all that his successor Philip V was able to accomplish, when, in 220 B.C., he had the Hellenic synod accept the repeated challenge of war offered to him by the Ætolians, who, taking advantage of the accession of a young and untried king to the throne of Macedon, assailed his hegemony in Greece while it

[1] Plut., *Aratus*, 45.   [2] Polybius, IV, 24.

was still precarious. Had Doson lived to wage the Social War (220–217 B.C.), he might have crushed the Ætolians by sheer weight of numbers, and have completed the unification of Hellas. Philip V fought bravely and skillfully and won the respect of both his friends and his foes; but before any definite issue of the struggle had arrived, the campaign between Hannibal and the Romans had reached such a point that the hegemon of Hellas dared not neglect it any longer.

"Let Greece," said Agelaus of Naupactus at the peace conference which followed,[1] "be united; let no Greek state make war upon any other; let them thank the Gods if they can all live in peace and agreement, if, as men in crossing rivers grasp one another's hands, so they can hold together and save themselves and their cities from barbarian inroads. If it is too much to hope that it should be so always, let it at least be so just now; let Greeks, now at least, unite and keep on their guard, when they behold the vastness of the armies and the greatness of the struggle going on in the West. No man who looks at the state of things with common care can doubt what is coming. Whether Rome conquers Carthage or Carthage conquers Rome, the victor will not be content with the dominion of the Greeks of Italy and Sicily; he will extend his plans and his warfare much further than suits us or our welfare. Let all Greece be

[1] Polybius, v. 104. (Translated by Freeman, *History of Federal Government*, pp. 435 f.)

on its guard, and Philip above all. Your truest defense, O King," he continued, "will be found in the character of the chief and protector of the Greeks. Leave off destroying Greek cities; leave off weakening them till they become a prey to every invader. Rather watch over Greece, as you watch over your own body; guard the interests of all her members as you guard the interest of what is your own. If you follow such a course as this, you will win the good will of Greece; you will have every Greek bound to you as a friend and as a sure supporter in all your undertakings; foreign powers will see the confidence which the whole nation reposes in you, and will fear to attack either you or them. If you wish for conquest and military glory, another field invites you. Cast your eyes to the West; look at the war raging in Italy; of that war you may easily, by a skilful policy, make yourself the arbiter; a blow dealt in time may make you master of both the contending powers. If you cherish such hopes, no time bids fairer than the present for their accomplishment. But as for disputes and wars with Greeks, put them aside till some season of leisure; let it be your main object to keep in your own hands the power of making war and peace with them when you will. If once the clouds which are gathering in the West should advance and spread over Greece and the neighboring lands, there will be danger indeed that all our truces and wars, all the child's play with which we now amuse ourselves, will be suddenly cut short. We may then pray in vain to the Gods for the power of making war and peace with one another, and indeed of dealing independently with any of the questions which may arise among us."

The speaker was right, and Philip took his advice. But when he became embroiled with Rome, it was the speaker's own countrymen, the Ætolians, who, by attacking Macedon in the rear, contributed most to the dreaded sequel: that never after 212 B.C. did the Greeks have an opportunity of dealing independently with any of the questions which arose among them. At the time of the Social War Macedon missed its last chance of establishing a single state in European Hellas.

SELECT BIBLIOGRAPHY

1. DROYSEN, J. G. *Geschichte des Hellenismus,*[2] III: *Geschichte der Epigonen* (1877).
2. FREEMAN, E. *History of Federal Government in Greece and Italy* [2] (1893). Ed. by J. B. Bury.
3. NIESE, B. *Geschichte der griechischen und makedonischen Staaten.* Especially vol. II (1899).
4. BELOCH, J. *Griechische Geschichte,* III (1904).
5. KÄRST, J. *Geschichte des hellenistischen Zeitalters,* II, I (1909).
6. FERGUSON, W. S. *Hellenistic Athens* (1911).
7. POZZI, EMILIO. *Le Battaglie di Cos e di Andro e la Politica marittima di Antigono Gonata.* In *Memorie della Reale Accademia delle Scienze di Torino:* serie II, tom. LXIII (1912).
8. TARN, W. W. *Antigonus Gonatas* (1913).

THE END

INDEX

INDEX

Absolutism, creation of, 135; legalized in Greece, 147 *f.*
Acarnania, 234.
Achæa. *See* League.
Ætolia. *See* League.
Agelaus of Naupactus, speech of, 246.
Agon, in Athens, 58 *ff.*
Alexander of Corinth, rebellion of, 230; death of, 232.
Alexander the Great, 4; deification of, 36; accession of, to throne, 116, 123 *f.*; character of, 119; training of, 119 *ff.*; and Aristotle, 119 *ff.*; love of symbolism of, 123, 128, 139; destroys Thebes, 123 *f.*; spares Pindar's house, 124; visits Troy, 124 *f.*; cuts Gordian knot, 125 *f.*; plan of Persian campaign of, 126 *f.*; son of Zeus, 128, 133, 162 *f.*; in Persepolis, 129; dissolves Hellenic league, 129 *f.*; ceases to be hegemon of Hellas, 130; ceases to be king of Macedon, 130 *f.*; marries Roxane, 130; adopts Persian costume, 130; tries to establish Hellenism in Asia, 133 *f.*; founds city-states, 134 *f.*; plans conquest of West, 134; and absolute monarchy, 135; changes opinion as to Iranians, 135 *f.*; tries to fuse dominant peoples of Europe and Asia, 136 *ff.*; marries Persian princesses, 137; plans of, 144, rejected by the Macedonians, 150; demands recognition as a god, 146; departs from the life among men, 149.
Alexandria, 155, 157, 163, 213; new Athens, 158; trade of, 161 *f.*; imperial cult of Ptolemies in, 164 *ff.*;

vs. Memphis, 170; laws of, 177; classes of population in, 181.
Ammon, god of Cyrene, 126 *ff.*; visited by Alexander, 139.
Ancient City, of Fustel de Coulanges, criticized, 7.
Andros, battle of, 159, 233.
Antigonids, constitutional government of, 216; wars of, with Rome, 217 *f.*; alliance of, with Seleucids, 223.
Antigonus I, Monophthalmus, 183; tries to take Alexander's place and fails, 184 *f.*; policy of, 218 *f.*; monarchy of, 220 *f.*
Antigonus II, Gonatas, victories of, at Cos and Andros, 159; rightful heir of Macedonian crown, 220; suzerain of Greece, 220; king of Macedon, 220, 223; education of, 222 *f.*; reign of, 223–233; peace of, with Egypt, 223; hostility of, with Epirus, 224; protects Greece from barbarians, 224; tyrants of, in Greece, 224 *ff.*; relation of, to Stoa, 225 *f.*; refuses deification, 225 *f.*; struggle of, with Ptolemy Philadelphus, 226, 229; renews alliance with Seleucids, 229; deserted by Antiochus II, 230; recovers Ægean, 232; treaty of, with Ætolians, 232; empire of, 233; death of, 233; failure of, in Greece, 235.
Antigonus III, Doson, Hellenic league of, 34; makes peace with Ætolians, 241; hegemon of Hellas, 243.
Antiochus I, Soter, 185.
Antiochus II, Theos, 185; deserts Macedon, 230.
Antiochus III, the Great, 187 *ff.*;

INDEX

INDEX — page **257**

Races, fusion of, in Seleucid empire, 206.

Reaction, age of, 95 *ff.*; of Plato, unreality of, 106 *f.*

Reformation, age of, in Greece, 83.

Reformers, political, 26.

Religion, and deification of rulers, 141 *f.*; in Egypt, 178 *f.*

Representation according to population, 27, 33 *f.*, 237, 243.

Rhodians, war of, with Ptolemy II, 229.

Romans, heirs of Greeks, 5; empire of, 35; save Ptolemies, 160; war of, with Illyrians, 241, with Macedonians, 248.

Rome, Senate of, disarms Seleucids, 190 *f.*, encourages revolt of Jews, 191, sets up usurpers in Syria, 191; emperors of, use Seleucid land policy, 204; Italian federation of, compared with Seleucid empire, 210 *f.*; intimidates Seleucids, 213 *f.*; imperial problems of, 214.

Rotation of office, in Athens, 55 *f.*

Roxane, married by Alexander, 130. 136.

Samians, get Athenian citizenship, 31.

Sarapis, 178.

Sea-power, benefits of, 66 *ff.*; gained by Alexander, 126 *f.*; of Egypt, 156, 158; struggle for, between Egypt and Macedon, 159; abandoned by Egypt, 160; first gained by Egypt, 227; restored, 230, lost, 233.

Seleucids, hemmed in by Egypt, 159; division in dynasty of, 187; get access to sea, 188; lose prestige in Asia, 189 *f.*; disarmed by Rome, 190 *f.*; dynastic war among, 191; half Iranian, 195; expansion of, 196 *ff.*; crown lands of, 199; land policy of, 202 *f.*; administrative service of, 203; local government of, 203, 205; empire of, a conglomerate

of states, 205 *ff.*; relation of, to city-states, 208; difficulties of, 211; intimidated by Rome, 213 *f.*

Seleucus, son of Antiochus, 184; at Ipsus, 185; reaches Mediterranean, 185; at Corupedion, 185; faithful to Iranian wife, 195; relation to Alexander, 195. . . . *Callinicus*, 186.

Sellasia, battle of, 242.

Semites, view of Alexander as to, 135 *f.*

Sicilian expedition, 76.

Sicyon, added to Achæan league, 230.

Siwah, oasis of, visited by Alexander, 126 *ff.*, 139 *ff.*

Slavery, rôle of, in Athens, 61 *f.*

Social War, 246.

Socrates, 97.

Sparta, size of, 19; Peloponnesian league of, 20; Hellenic league of, 20 *f.*; supports aristocracy, 20; pretexts of, for tyranny, 25; refuses to enter Achæan league, 32 *f.*; funeral custom of, 43; home of poets and musicians, 81 *f.*; golden age of art at, 82; absence of tyrants in, 84; military life of, 84 *f.*; puritan movement in, 85; army of, 86; danger of, from Helots, 87; growth of, 87 *ff.*; change of foreign policy by, 88 *f.*; in conflict with democratic movement, 89 *f.*; domestic situation in, when hegemon, 90 *ff.*; imperial problems of, 93 *ff* ; donation to, from Ætolians, 241.

Spartans, kinsmen of the Jews, 79 *f.*

Stasis, 22 *ff.*

Stoa, philosophy of, in Macedon, 225 *f.*

Superiority, essential in empire, 2.

Susa, great marriage of, 136 *ff.*

Symmachia, basis of Spartan empire, 20 *f.*; of Athenian empire, 24 *f.*

Sympolity, defined, 32 *f.*

The Riverside Press
CAMBRIDGE · MASSACHUSETTS
PRINTED IN THE U.S.A.